GOVERNMENT PROCEDURES AND OPERATIONS

A JOURNALIST'S GUIDE TO COVERING FEDERAL COURTS

Government Procedures and Operations

Additional books in this series can be found on Nova's website under the Series tab.

Additional e-books in this series can be found on Nova's website under the e-book tab.

GOVERNMENT PROCEDURES AND OPERATIONS

A JOURNALIST'S GUIDE TO COVERING FEDERAL COURTS

LILLIANA JONES
EDITOR

New York

Library of Congress Cataloging-in-Publication Data

ISBN: 978-1-63463-382-6

Published by Nova Science Publishers, Inc. † New York

CONTENTS

Preface

Reporting about a federal trial court or appellate court is quite unlike reporting on the other two branches of government. Among the most notable differences are that some legal terms are hard to understand; there are many rules; and federal judges work largely alone. This book provides a guide for journalists on federal courts. It also provides an analytic overview of the professional experiences and qualifications of those individuals who are currently serving as active U.S. circuit court judges; provides a statistical analysis of the time from nomination to confirmation for U.S. circuit and district court nominees from Presidents Reagan to Obama; identifies possible consequences of a protracted confirmation process for circuit and district court nominees; and identifies policy options the Senate might consider to shorten the length of time from nomination to confirmation for lower federal court nominees.

Chapter 1 – Federal judges and the journalists who cover them share much common ground. One clear area of mutual interest is accurate and informed coverage of federal courts. A Journalist's Guide to the Federal Courts is intended to assist reporters assigned to court coverage. It is the media who inform and educate the public about the courts, spark discussion and debate about their work, instill public trust and confidence in the institution and its function, and help protect judicial independence. These are worthwhile and important pursuits.

There are justifiable and distinct differences between the three branches of government and the access they grant the news media. Most of the work of federal courts is performed in open court and decisions, and in most cases court filings are available on the Internet. This primer is aimed at helping reporters who cover federal appellate, district, and bankruptcy courts – the cases, the people, and the process.

Chapter 2 – This report provides an analysis of the professional qualifications and experiences of U.S. circuit court judges who are currently serving on the federal bench. Interest in the professional qualifications of those nominated to the federal judiciary has been demonstrated by Congress and others. Congressional interest in the professional experiences of those nominated by a President to the federal courts reflects, in part, the evaluative role of Congress in examining the qualifications of those who are nominated to life-tenure positions. Other organizations, such as the American Bar Association (ABA), also have an ongoing interest in the professional qualifications of those appointed to the federal judiciary. Additionally, scholars have demonstrated an interest in this topic by examining whether a relationship exists between the professional or career experiences of judges and judicial decision making.

Chapter 3 – The process by which lower federal court judges are nominated by the President and considered by the Senate is of continuing interest to Congress. Recent Senate debate over judicial nominations has frequently concerned whether a particular President's judicial nominees, relative to the nominees of other recent Presidents, waited longer for their nominations to be considered by the Senate. This report addresses this issue by (1) providing a statistical analysis of the time from nomination to confirmation for U.S. circuit and district court nominees from Presidents Reagan to Obama; (2) identifying possible consequences of a protracted confirmation process for circuit and district court nominees; and (3) identifying policy options the Senate might consider to shorten the length of time from nomination to confirmation for lower federal court nominees. In general, the mean (average) and median number of days from nomination to confirmation increased during each presidency since President Reagan. For circuit court nominees confirmed during a President's time in office (whether one or two terms), the average number of days elapsed from nomination to confirmation ranged from 68.7 days during the Reagan presidency to 350.6 days during George W. Bush's presidency. The median number of days from nomination to confirmation for circuit court nominees confirmed ranged from 45 days (Reagan) to 229 days (Obama). For district court nominees, the average time between nomination and confirmation ranged from 67.9 days (Reagan) to 220.8 days (Obama). For district court nominees, the median time elapsed ranged from a low of 41 days (Reagan) to 215 days (Obama). There are several potential consequences of a protracted confirmation process for lower federal court nominees. These include (1) consistently high vacancy rates for circuit and district court judgeships as well as a greater number of such vacancies considered "judicial emergencies" by the Judicial Conference of the United States; (2) detrimental effects on the management of the federal courts, including judicial caseloads; (3) greater difficulty in finding highly qualified individuals who are willing to be nominated to the federal bench; (4) the politicization of the confirmation process in a manner that might leave the public with the impression that the ideological or partisan predisposition of the nominee is the primary consideration in determining how the nominee will approach his or her work on the bench. Three policy options discussed in the report include the following: Utilizing time frames for various stages of the confirmation process for U.S. circuit and district court nominees, including the length of time from nomination to committee hearing as well as the length of time from committee report to final Senate action. Expediting the confirmation process for judicial nominations using "fast-track" procedures. Such procedures might include classifying some judicial nominations as "privileged nominations" as is currently done to expedite Senate consideration of nominations to some positions in the executive branch. Treating district court nominations differently than circuit court nominations by changing certain features of the confirmation process for district court nominations. Such changes might result in shortening the time from nomination to confirmation for district court nominees.

In: A Journalist's Guide …
Editor: Lilliana Jones

ISBN: 978-1-63463-382-6

Chapter 1

A JOURNALIST'S GUIDE TO FEDERAL COURTS*

Administrative Office of the United States Courts

WELCOME TO FEDERAL COURT

This guide assumes you have a basic understanding of the U.S. legal system. If not, you may want to peruse "Understanding the Federal Courts," a publication of the Administrative Office of the U.S. Courts (http:// www.uscourts.gov/EducationalResources/FederalCourtBasics/UnderstandingTheFederalCourts.aspx). The Administrative Office, based in Washington, D.C., is the federal Judiciary's central support agency, providing various services to federal courts. It has an Office of Public Affairs, 202-502-2600, which may be able to help you. You may also want to explore other features, including an online version of this Guide, on the Judiciary's web site, www.uscourts.gov.

Whether you're reporting about a high-profile case or your new full-time beat is the federal courthouse, you'll find that covering a federal trial court or appellate court is quite unlike reporting on the other two branches of government. Among the most notable differences:

- **Some legal terms are hard to understand.** You don't need a law degree to cover the federal courts, but a big part of your job will be

* This is an edited, reformatted and augmented version of a publication issued in 2011.

translating legal jargon and procedures for your readers or viewers. This guide should help. When in doubt, check out the guide's glossary or another reference tool.

- **Rules. Rules. Rules.** There are layers upon layers of rules: Rules that govern all federal cases; rules that govern all cases in your local federal court; rules that govern all cases before a particular judge. Understanding the rules – and their exceptions – will greatly inform your coverage.
- **Judges do their own work.** Federal judges work largely alone. Each judge has law clerks, who usually join the court for one year soon after graduation from law school. They assist with legal research and may help draft sections of opinions or orders, but judges make the decisions and take the leading role in explaining them.

Insiders often refer to **district court judges** and **appellate court judges** as Article III judges, because their terms of service are governed by Article III of the U.S. Constitution (http://www.archives.gov/exhibits/charters/constitution_transcript.html). They are nominated by the President and confirmed by the U.S. Senate. **Bankruptcy judges** are not Article III judges. They are not appointed by the president, but by the courts of appeals. There are no constitutional requirements to serve as a federal judge, but in modern times all judges have been lawyers.

Like the Supreme Court justices, federal circuit and district judges serve for life, provided they exhibit good behavior. They can be removed from office only by a trial of impeachment in the U.S. Senate. Their salaries, which are set by Congress, cannot be reduced while they are in office. All appellate court judges receive the same salary, no matter where they serve. The same is true for district court judges.

Each district court judge sits in one of the 94 federal judicial districts. There is at least one judicial district in every state, the District of Columbia and Puerto Rico. The territorial courts in the Virgin Islands, Guam and the Northern Marianna Islands have judges appointed for 10-year terms rather than for life. Each district may have multiple divisions. Each division typically has its own courthouse and judges hearing cases that arise in that particular geographic location. There are formal names of U.S. district courts. For instance: U.S. District Court for the Southern District of New York. "Manhattan federal trial court" is how a reporter might shorten it.

Each district court is located within one of the nation's 12 regional judicial circuits. The 12 regional courts of appeals serve as intermediate courts in the federal system, and are required to hear any appeal brought at the conclusion of a district court case by a criminal defendant or by the losing party in a civil action. Decisions of the courts of appeals may be reviewed by the U.S. Supreme Court, but the nation's highest court has total discretion to determine whether it will hear the appeal. It grants full review only to a tiny percentage of the cases that reach it each year.

Senior judges are partially retired Article III judges. There is no requirement that judges take senior status because there is no mandatory retirement age for Article III judges. Judges are eligible to take senior status if they are at least 65 and have at least 15 years on the bench, or any combination of age and years of service thereafter that equals 80. Senior judges continue to draw their former salary, but may handle a reduced caseload. They are required to handle at least one-fourth of the workload of an active judge to qualify for future salary increases. By taking senior status, even if maintaining a full caseload, a judge creates a vacancy on the court, to be filled by the nomination/confirmation process.

Visiting judges, like senior judges, can help a court stay on top of its caseload. Visiting judges have long provided significant assistance to courts they visit. Article III judges may sit by designation and assignment in any other federal court having a need for their services. They provide temporary assistance not only when a court's own judges must disqualify themselves, but also to help meet the caseload needs arising from vacancies, lack of sufficient judgeships, specific emergencies, and other workload imbalances.

COVERING FEDERAL DISTRICT COURT

The best journalists who cover the federal courts distinguish themselves by their knowledge of the intricacies of the system. They find documents other reporters overlook, they understand documents that other reporters misinterpret, and they anticipate what's coming next.

This chapter will walk through each stage of both a criminal and a civil case. But first, it describes the key players in the federal trial courts. It also identifies the types of court information you'll need and the possible sources for that information.

Key Players

The district court's **chief judge** position is assigned based on length of service. It is held by the longest-serving active judge from among those judges who are 64 years old or younger, have served for one year or more as a judge, and have not previously served as chief judge. The chief judge serves for a term of seven years or to age 70, whatever comes first, and handles administrative matters related to operation of the clerk's office and the courthouse that do not require the attention of all the judges. He or she generally carries a full caseload in addition to administrative duties. A chief judge does not receive any additional pay.

> Senior judges are a major part of the federal Judiciary. They handle 15-20 percent of district court and appellate court cases.

Magistrate judges are appointed by the U.S. district judges in each judicial district for a term of service of eight years (four years for part-time magistrate judges), which can be renewed. They hear the federal equivalent of misdemeanor cases – minor crimes committed on federal lands. They also handle preliminary matters in criminal cases, and are usually the first judicial officer a defendant sees following arrest or indictment. In most districts, magistrate judges also handle pretrial motions and hearings in civil cases and felony criminal cases; those cases are eventually turned over to district judges for trial. Magistrate judges may preside over civil trials if the parties consent. The job title is magistrate judge, not magistrate.

Each federal judicial district has a **clerk of court** whose staff, among other duties, accepts papers and electronic filings and moves those paper or electronic documents from the clerk's office to judges' chambers. The clerk's office serves as the court's central nervous system –all matters must flow through it, and the clerk of court serves as custodian of the record in every case. The staff members you will deal with at the front counter of the clerk's office are generally referred to as **docket clerks**. Most districts with multiple divisions also have two or more **division managers**, who supervise clerk's office staff in a given courthouse. Because they function primarily as supervisors and managers, you may rarely see the clerk of court or division manager in a courtroom.

In each judge's courtroom, generally seated in front of the judge's bench, is the **courtroom deputy clerk**. In addition to being the person primarily responsible for maintaining the case files, the courtroom deputy clerk calls cases at the beginning of a hearing, swears in witnesses during trials, and receives exhibits introduced into evidence at trial. The courtroom deputy clerk is a member of the clerk's office staff, not a member of the judge's personal staff, and should not be confused with the judge's **law clerks**, who generally also sit near the judge's bench during hearings. It is a courtroom deputy clerk who generally announces the arrival of the judge in the courtroom, sometimes by saying, "All rise. Oyez, oyez, oyez . . ."

> "Oyez" means "hear ye" in the Anglo-Norman language used in the courts of Medieval England.

Court reporters generally sit in front of the judge, facing the attorneys. They are responsible for recording the proceedings, either by using a stenographic machine or an audio recording hood, which looks like a mask, into which they repeat the words spoken during the hearing. They typically are employed by the court, and are paid a salary for recording hearings and trials, and providing copies of transcripts to the judge and the clerk of court. All parties, journalists, and members of the public who want a copy of the transcript must pay the reporter a per-page fee, which is set by the Judicial Conference of the United States.

Federal court policy states that transcripts created by court reporters or transcribers will be made available for inspection and copying in a clerk of court's office and for download from the PACER public access service 90 days after they are delivered to the clerk. Individuals will be able to view, download, or print a copy of a transcript from PACER for eight cents per page. During the 90-day period, transcripts will be available at the clerk's office for inspection only, or may be purchased from the court reporter or transcriber. The per-page fee charged is set by the Judicial Conference of the United States.

In courthouses, you will see two kinds of security personnel. Each federal judicial district has a United States Marshal, who is appointed by the President and reports to the attorney general. The marshal oversees the security of the district court. (http://www.usdoj.gov/marshals) He or she heads an office of **deputy U.S. marshals**, who typically wear business attire when in the courtroom, are responsible for the custody and transportation of prisoners, and the safety of witnesses, jurors, and the judge. There typically are two or more deputy marshals present whenever a criminal defendant who is being detained during the trial is present in the courtroom. Outside the courtroom, the U.S. Marshals Service runs the Witness Security Program, which is more commonly known as the witness protection program, in which witnesses who could face retribution are relocated under new identities after they testify. The U.S.M.S. is also the federal government's lead agency in tracking down fugitives.

> Journalists should never cross from the spectator gallery into the well of the courtroom, which is generally marked by a short rail, without seeking permission from the judge or a court employee.

Court security officers, who dress in blue blazers and gray pants, also work under the direction of the U.S. Marshal. They are responsible for the safety of the public in the courthouse. They staff the metal detectors inside the front doors of most courthouses. Generally at least one court security officer – also known as a CSO – is present at every court hearing.

Each federal judicial district has a U.S. Attorney's Office (http://www.usdoj.gov/usao/offices/index.html), which is the local office of the U.S. Department of Justice. The **U.S. attorney**, who runs the office, is nominated by the President and confirmed by the U.S. Senate for a four-year term. **Assistant U.S. attorneys** ordinarily serve as the government's lawyers in both criminal and civil cases. In criminal cases, they often are joined at the courtroom's counsel table by the lead **law enforcement agent** who investigated the case. Assistant U.S. attorneys are sometimes assisted by counsel from other federal agencies if the case involves an investigation that was begun by those agencies.

Representing defendants in a criminal case is one or more **defense counsel**. Defense counsel almost always sit at the table located the farthest from the jury box. If defendants can afford to, they are required to hire **private counsel**, unless the defendants choose to represent themselves. (Self-representation is known by the Latin term, appearing *pro se*.)

If defendants cannot afford an attorney, one will be appointed for them from one of two sources. **Federal public defenders** are government-paid lawyers who represent financially qualified defendants. **Criminal Justice Act (CJA) or panel attorneys** are lawyers in private practice who make themselves available to be appointed to represent such defendants. CJA attorneys are used in cases in which the federal public defender has a conflict of interest, representing one of several defendants in the same case. CJA attorneys also are used when public defenders do not have the resources – either staff or time – to handle the case, or if the particular court does not have a defender office. CJA attorneys generally are assigned at random from a list maintained by the clerk's office. In most judicial districts, however, judges can order that a particular attorney be assigned to a case if complexity of the case or the interests of justice require it.

Types and Sources of Court Information

First, a Word about Judges as Sources

When a question about a case arises, a journalist's natural instinct is to call the judge handling the matter. After all, who could provide a more accurate, authoritative answer? This is almost always a bad idea.

Federal judges are bound by the Code of Conduct for United States Judges, which requires that they "avoid public comment on the merits of pending or impending actions" in cases before them or on appeal. You can find the Code online at http://www.uscourts.gov/RulesAndPolicies/ CodesOf Conduct/CodeConductUnitedStatesJudges.aspx. Some federal judges will respond, or have a court employee respond, to a journalist's questions about procedural aspects of a case, but some judges refuse to be interviewed by journalists on any topic. (The same rules will apply to those judges' secretaries and law clerks.)

That is not to say you can never speak with a federal judge. Many judges speak at or attend bar association programs and other public events, at which it is perfectly appropriate to introduce yourself. Some also will talk informally to journalists about non case-related matters. If you are new to covering a federal court, it would not hurt to call the judge's chambers and ask if you can drop by simply to say hello.

So Who's Your Go-To Source?

If the judge is off-limits, to whom do you turn? Particularly if the federal courthouse is your full-time beat, you'll need someone when all other sources of information fail. That person probably works in the clerk's office.

A few courts have public information officers (PIOs) who deal with the news media on a daily basis. Most courts, however, do not have such an officer. Absent a PIO, the district executive, clerk of court or division manager should be able to help. They often designate a member of the clerk's staff, or some other court employee, as a contact person for the news media. For routine information about a case – when's the next hearing date, for instance – the docket clerks who staff the clerk's office front counter may be your best sources. But keep in mind that even these sources have their limits. It's not their job to talk about the substance of a case – such as the meaning of a ruling or how the charges in an indictment can be defended against. They provide access to court documents, schedules, pretrial hearings, and trials. They do not interpret those documents and proceedings.

> For questions about legal substance, start with the lawyers in the case. If they won't talk, call lawyers who have handled similar cases in your courthouse or professors at a local law school.

The Court's Docket

If you are the federal court beat reporter, you will need to keep abreast of all the noteworthy cases on the court's docket. Every district court has a web site (http://www.uscourts.gov/Court_Locator/CourtLocatorSearch.aspx), and some include a schedule of trials, motion hearings, pleas, and arraignments. Otherwise, you will need to visit the clerk's office on a daily basis to see the schedule. Many courts keep it in a large day planner on the front desk of the clerk's office.

Each court also keeps a list of all criminal and civil cases filed by date. They are often referred to as "the running lists." The Party/Case Locator on the PACER public access service provides electronic indices of cases in every federal district court. (See description of PACER in Pleadings, Orders, and Opinions section below.)

If you're only following a single high-profile case, your task is much easier. Early in the case, the judge will issue a scheduling order, setting out the dates motion papers must be filed, pretrial hearings will be held, and the trial will start.

Pleadings, Orders, and Opinions

All federal trial courts have computerized dockets. The docket lists the date and a brief description of all filings by the parties and all actions by the court in a particular case. You can access the dockets free of charge at terminals in the clerk's office.

The federal courts' Case Management/Electronic Case Files system provides enhanced and updated docket management, allowing courts to maintain case documents in electronic form. A growing number of courts use the system to permit lawyers to file case documents---pleadings, motions, petitions – with the court over the Internet.

The feature also allows the public to view the full text of those pleadings over the Internet through the Public Access to Court Electronic Records service (www.pacer.gov). PACER is current as of the previous day's close of business. It may not help if you need to report about a filing the day it occurs. The charge for looking at and printing out documents in PACER is minimal – eight cents per page of information, with a cap of $2.40 no matter how long a document is. Users of PACER need to register for a password that will allow access to the system.

If there is no electronic access to the full text of pleadings and opinions in your court, your only other option is the paper case file itself. It normally is in the clerk's office, but a few days before the trial begins, it may be sent to the judge's chambers for the duration of the case. You will be out of luck unless you can persuade a court employee to track it down and let you borrow it for a few minutes. Sometimes, attorneys involved in the case will provide you with copies of relevant case documents.

For cases that draw massive amounts of media attention, some courts have found it is more efficient to post the case documents on their web sites, providing free access. A court web site can automatically send reporters e-mails whenever a new document is added to the high-profile case's docket.

Reporters working on daily deadlines should know the difference between filing and docketing a document. Filing occurs when the document is handed over by the lawyer to the clerk's office to be time/date stamped as being received. Docketing occurs when notice of its filing is added to the case docket by a clerk's office staff. In most clerk's offices, a document is considered public information once it has been docketed. (A lag – of a few minutes to more than a day – can exist between filing and docketing.) If time is of the essence, you may want to get documents directly from the lawyers as soon as they are filed, rather than waiting for them to be docketed by staff in the clerk's office. Be aware, however, that in most instances a document will not be considered part of the court's official record until it appears on the docket.

Court Rules

Each district and bankruptcy court has its own set of local rules, which address procedural matters not uniformly governed by the Federal Rules of Procedure. In some jurisdictions, individual judges also have a set of rules that govern the cases in their courtrooms. Both are generally posted on the court's web site.

The court's local rules, in particular, often contain important information about covering the courthouse. For instance, a growing number of federal courts have banned cell phones, pagers, Palm Pilots, and Blackberry devices from their courthouses.

During the course of a case, you will hear and read references to a variety of other rules. The Federal Rules of Criminal Procedure, Federal Rules Civil Procedure, Federal Rules of Bankruptcy Procedure, and Federal Rules of Evidence set forth the general procedural requirements for litigating cases in federal courts. You also will need to be familiar with some federal laws, which are collected in the United States Code. Provisions of the United States Constitution also may be mentioned.

Federal Rules of Criminal Procedure - http://www.uscourts.gov/RulesAndPolicies/FederalRulemaking/Overview/CriminalRules. aspx

Federal Rules of Civil Procedure - http://www.uscourts.gov/RulesAndPolicies/FederalRulemaking/Overview/CivilRules.aspx

Federal Rules of Bankruptcy Procedure - http://www.uscourts.gov/RulesAndPolicies/FederalRulemaking/Overview/BankruptcyRules. aspx

Federal Rules of Evidence - http://www.uscourts.gov/RulesAndPolicies/FederalRulemaking/Overview/EvidenceRules. aspx

United States Code - http://www.gpoaccess.gov/uscode/

United States Constitution - http://www.archives.gov/national_archives_experience/charters/constitution.html

Sealing of Documents

Although neither the Freedom of Information Act nor the Privacy Act applies to the Judiciary, information received by the court is publicly available unless sealed by statute, rule, or order of the court.

Statutes provide for sealing documents in specific proceedings, such as juvenile and grand jury proceedings. More generally, a federal rule of civil procedure provides for protective orders during discovery to protect a party or person from annoyance, embarrassment, oppression, or undue burden or expense. Similarly, bankruptcy court records are public and open to examination except that the court may protect commercial information or protect a person "with respect to scandalous or defamatory matter."

There are no statutes or federal rules that provide guidance for when a court should or should not seal documents in cases not specifically covered by a statute or a rule. Courts sometimes have sealed documents that contain sensitive material, such as classified information affecting national security.

An entire case may be sealed at the opening of a case, or certain docket entries may be sealed during the course of the proceedings. These cases or documents generally are listed on the docket but with the notation that the information is sealed.

Judges' Biographical Information

The Federal Judicial Center, which is the federal court's educational and research agency, lists on its web site brief biographies of all Article III judges since the country was founded (http://www.fjc.gov/history/home.nsf/page/judges.html).

Broadcasting the Trial

Trials and other courtroom proceedings are generally open to the public. No federal trial court, however, permits broadcasting of its proceedings.

The biggest stumbling block to broadcasting federal trials is Federal Rule of Criminal Procedure 53, which says the court shall not permit the taking of photographs in the courtroom during judicial proceedings or the broadcasting of judicial proceedings from the courtroom. Members of Congress on occasion have introduced bills that would give federal trial judges the discretion to allow broadcasting trials. To date, none has been enacted.

There are two types of exceptions to this prohibition that are worth noting, though neither provides video for public broadcast:

- In the trial of Timothy McVeigh, who was charged with bombing the Oklahoma City Federal Building in 1995, Congress passed a law that required the federal court hearing the case in Denver to set up a closed-circuit viewing location for relatives of the victims in Oklahoma City.
- In cases where a single courtroom will not hold all spectators, some federal courts, at the presiding judge's discretion, have piped a closed-circuit video feed of the proceedings into an adjacent room, which can double or triple the number of spectators accommodated.

You will need to check where, if anywhere, in the courthouse you are allowed to have a cell phone, pager, tape recorder, or other electronic device.

The policy-making Judicial Conference of the United States in 2010 allowed district and bankruptcy courts to make those digital audio recordings of courtroom proceedings, at the discretion of the presiding judge, available online to the public through PACER at $2.40 per audio file. Previously, such access was possible only by obtaining a CD recording from a court clerk's office for $26. Digital audio recording is used in most bankruptcy courts and a growing number of district courts (where magistrate judges account for most of the usage).

A Criminal Case

The Investigation

A defendant may be arrested in the course of allegedly committing a crime. But the criminal cases that attract media attention most often involve a protracted investigation prior to a defendant's arrest. The investigation will generally be conducted by the FBI, but other federal agencies may be involved depending on the nature of the alleged crime (DEA for drug investigations, SEC for securities investigations, etc.).

To obtain a search warrant or arrest warrant, the law enforcement agent and an assistant U.S. attorney will have to make an application to a magistrate judge or district court judge. The applications will be accompanied by an affidavit filed by the lead law enforcement agent, which is meant to provide the judge with evidence of probable cause. Both documents can be valuable for reporters. The application itself – a one-page form – will include information about the defendant, and the affidavit will include an overview of the facts of the case.

To avoid public disclosure of the investigation, search warrant applications generally are sealed, at least until the search is conducted and sometimes until after the arrest is made. While they are sealed, the warrant application will typically show up on the court's docket under a title that gives away nothing about the substance of the case, such as "*In re search warrant application*."

But if a search warrant application is unsealed before an arrest, that provides a valuable lead that an investigation is underway. Courthouse beat reporters should review unsealed warrants on a regular basis. The ways that clerk's offices file search warrant applications vary greatly from office to office; you'll have to ask at your courthouse about the easiest way to routinely review the documents.

Prosecutors use three terms to describe people involved in investigations, and it is critical that you distinguish among them. A "witness" is someone who merely has information useful to the investigation. A "subject" of an investigation is a person whose conduct is within the scope of a criminal probe, although they themselves may not be suspected of breaking the law. A "target" is someone who is likely to be indicted. A subject of an investigation can become a target.

Indictment

Before the target of an investigation is arrested, prosecutors generally will take the evidence they have gathered to a grand jury. Grand juries are composed of 16 to 23 citizens. Agreement by a bare majority is required to find probable cause exists that a crime was committed.

Grand juries are formally supervised by a district judge, often the chief judge, but for all practical purposes they function day-to-day under the auspices of the U.S. Attorney's Office. Only prosecutors present evidence before a grand jury, and a finding of probable cause – necessary to issue an indictment – is a relatively low standard of proof.

The indictment lists the crimes the defendant allegedly committed and describes the facts the government believes support those allegations. It is a roadmap to what the prosecution intends to prove at trial. Grand jury indictments are returned to the district court – usually to a magistrate judge – in a sealed court hearing. Indictments generally are unsealed after a defendant is arrested.

A criminal case also can begin without an indictment. In these cases, the lead investigator swears out a criminal complaint, called an "information," setting forth the same kinds of allegations and facts that would be contained in an indictment. Absent an indictment, the prosecution must convince a judge that there is probable cause to proceed with the case.

These hearings are held in open court after the defendant has been arrested in a felony case. A defendant can agree to waive indictment and proceed with the case based on the criminal complaint, or can demand that the prosecutor seek an indictment.

Defendant Appears in Court

Within hours of the defendant's arrest, he or she will make an **initial appearance** in court. Defendants are typically not represented by counsel at this hearing. They are advised of the charges they face, their rights are explained to them by the judge, and counsel is appointed if defendants cannot afford to hire their own lawyer. Defendants will be remanded to the custody of the U.S. Marshals Service at the conclusion of this hearing unless they are released, in which case conditions of release will be set.

Defendants are provided with the services of a court interpreter in all courtroom appearances when language is a barrier to the effective administration of justice.

If no indictment has been issued, the defendant will next have a **preliminary examination hearing**, at which the government will present its evidence. If the judge finds there is probable cause (or if an indictment has already been returned), there will then be a **detention hearing**, where it will be determined whether the defendant needs to be held in jail until trial. Both sides may present evidence at this hearing, as well as cross-examine the other side's witnesses.

> The likelihood the defendant will flee and the danger they pose to the community are the only two factors a judge may consider in a detention hearing.

The decision whether to release the defendant is governed by the Bail Reform Act of 1984 and subsequent amendments to it. The law presumes that defendants should be released on personal recognizance or unsecured personal bond (that is, without putting up any money or other asset as security) unless the judge determines "that such release will not reasonably assure the appearance of the person as required or will endanger the safety of any other person or the community."

The judge can put restrictions on defendants – such as requiring a secured bond, forfeiture of a passport, electronic monitoring of defendants' location, requiring they remain in their home, etc. But the judge must choose "the least restrictive . . . condition, or combination of conditions, that . . . will reasonably assure the appearance of the person as required and the safety of any other person and the community."

There are exceptions to the presumption that defendants should be released pending trial. The Act creates a rebuttable presumption that defendants should not be released under the following circumstances:

- The defendant is accused of one of a list of crimes listed in the statute, and was previously convicted of committing one of the specified crimes while free on bail.
- The judge finds there is probable cause the defendant committed a federal drug offense that carries a penalty of 10 years or more in prison.
- The judge finds there is probable cause the defendant used a firearm to commit a felony.

To rebut the presumption and release a defendant, the judge must find that some condition or combination of conditions of release will assure defendants' appearance at trial and safeguard the community.

> Pretrial reports are always filed under seal, but they often are discussed at length during the detention hearing.

Prior to the detention hearing, a member of the court's Pretrial Services office will speak to the defendant and as many family members as possible. The officer will file a report with the judge, prosecutor, and defense counsel that makes a recommendation whether the defendant can be released and, if so, under what conditions. This is a recommendation only, and it is not binding on the judge.

A decision to release or detain a defendant that is made by a magistrate judge may be reviewed by a district judge on the motion of either party. (This is a kind of appeal, though the word "appeal" is not used to describe it.) Detention orders may also be appealed to the court of appeals after a district judge rules on them.

The last of the early hearings in a criminal case is the **arraignment**. The defendant's counsel is asked three questions:

- Does the defendant waive a formal arraignment, at which the indictment would be read in its entirety?
- How does the defendant plead, guilty or not guilty?
- Does the defendant request a trial by jury? (If not, the case will be decided by the judge in what is known as a bench trial.)

If a formal arraignment is waived – as it almost always is – the hearing can be over in five minutes.

At the arraignment, some judges also schedule the trial date and dates for motion hearings. Under the Speedy Trial Act, criminal defendants are entitled to a trial that begins no later than 70 days from the date the indictment or information was filed, or from the date the defendant appears before a judge, whichever is later. The defendant can waive the right to a speedy trial, or the judge can waive the requirements of the Act by finding that the interests of justice require it.

These four hearings can be held at a single time under certain circumstances. In some courts magistrate judges hold all of these hearings; in other courts, some are held by magistrate judges while others are held by District Court judges. In most courts, the District Court judge who will handle the trial is assigned to the case after the initial appearance; check with the clerk's office for that judge's name. Judges are assigned to cases at random, to avoid the possibility that prosecutors might "judge shop" their case to a jurist considered friendly to prosecution arguments.

Pretrial Motions and Hearings

A wide variety of motions may be made prior to trial. Among the most common that are filed by the defense are:

- Motions to relocate the trial through a change of venue, claiming pretrial publicity will make it impossible to select an impartial jury.
- Motions challenging the admissibility of certain pieces of evidence.
- Motions seeking access to evidence in the possession of the prosecution.

This phase of the case, known as motion practice, occurs primarily on paper. Only if a judge feels that oral argument of the issues or evidence from witnesses would aid in a decision will a hearing be held.

During the pretrial phase, you also may encounter efforts to seal what hearings there are. Most pretrial hearings must be open to the public, but there are a complicated set of exceptions. Media organizations may decide to oppose the sealing of court records.

Plea Bargains and Sentencing

More than 90 percent of federal defendants plead guilty. Some do so during the pretrial phase as part of a plea bargain, in exchange for the prosecutors' dropping some charges or recommending a more lenient sentence.

Two documents are filed with the court at the plea hearing: the plea agreement, which outlines what charges are being pleaded to and which are being dropped; and a statement of facts describing what the defendant admits to doing. Both generally are available only after the hearing has ended.

During the hearing, the judge will conduct what is known as the plea colloquy, in which defendants are informed of the rights they are giving up and the crimes they are admitting. At some point, the judge will ask the defendants to, in their words, describe what they did.

Sentencing is generally scheduled for a month or more after the plea hearing, to allow time for the staff of the court's Probation Office to prepare a presentence investigation report. The probation officer will speak to the defendant, family members, friends, and others as part of the investigation. The report is always filed with the judge, prosecutor, and defense counsel under seal. Starting in 1987, sentencing in federal court was governed by the U.S. Sentencing Guidelines. They are set by the U.S. Sentencing Commission (http://www.ussc.gov), a judicial branch agency created by Congress to make sentencing more determinate and lessen sentencing disparities. In January 2005, the U.S. Supreme Court ruled that the guidelines are merely advisory. Judges are urged to consider the guidelines but now can depart from the guideline ranges, so long as the sentence is reasonable and does not exceed the maximum term set by statute for a particular crime.

The presentence report makes a recommendation as to how the guidelines rate the seriousness of the offense and the defendant's criminal history. Prosecutors and defense counsel will have made a similar estimate when they agreed to the plea bargain. The judge is not required to follow the recommendations of the Probation Office or the parties. During the sentencing hearing, defendants are given a chance to tell the court anything they believe the judge should consider before imposing sentence.

The Trial

Jury Selection

During jury selection, which is also known as voir dire, the lawyers, the judge or both will question prospective jurors about their backgrounds and their ability to be impartial. Prospective jurors may be struck from the panel in two ways. Lawyers may exercise a "challenge for cause," claiming the juror could not be impartial. If the judge agrees, the potential juror is excused. "Peremptory challenges" allow lawyers to remove a juror without stating a reason. Both sides are given a limited number of these peremptory challenges.

> Federal criminal juries typically have 12 members, plus up to six alternate jurors. To insure everyone pays attention to the testimony, no juror knows which of them are alternates until they are excused after closing arguments.

Jury selection in death penalty and other complex cases can take several weeks. In some courts, judges handling a high- profile trial will call in 200 or more jurors to fill out an extensive questionnaire, and then call in 20 or more a day to be questioned individually and challenged for cause. On the final day of jury selection in such cases, the qualified pool of jurors is called in, both sides exercise their peremptory challenges, and the jury is seated.

You should never contact a prospective juror or his or her family or close friends, nor should you speak about the case if you know you are in the presence of a juror while a case is active. This is considered jury tampering – a crime.

In cases in which judges are concerned about the safety of jurors, the jury may be anonymous, identified only by numbers. No one, other than the person in the clerk's office who arranges their payment (jurors are paid $40 per day), will know their names in such a case. A judge may decide that a need exists to sequester a jury – keep all jurors in the court's custody until a trial concludes.

Opening Statements

It is opening *statements* and closing *arguments*. At the beginning of a trial, lawyers are limited to telling the jury what they believe the evidence will show. Only at the end can they marshal those facts to make an argument the defendant did or did not commit the crime.

Prosecutors go first because they bear the burden of proving beyond a reasonable doubt that the defendant committed the crime. Defense counsel are not obligated to make an opening statement or present any evidence, since the defendant is presumed innocent. Defense counsel may choose to make an opening statement at the conclusion of the initial set of prosecution witnesses, known as the prosecution's case-in-chief.

Testimony, Exhibits, and Transcripts

Some individual judges or local rules of court require the prosecution to file a list of potential witnesses prior to trial, along with a list of exhibits that may be entered into evidence. These lists can provide a handy reference for reporters. Check the case file about a week before trial begins.

Prosecution witnesses take the stand first. Each can be cross-examined by the defense. If a witness is cross-examined, the prosecution is permitted a "redirect," asking the witness only questions related to the topics discussed during cross-examination. You are free to speak to witnesses after they are excused by the court, unless the judge indicates the witness is subject to recall to the stand later in the trial. The witness, however, is not obligated to respond to your questions, and often may be advised by counsel not to do so.

At the end of the prosecution's case-in-chief, the defense likely will make what is known as a Rule 29 motion. Named after Federal Rule of Criminal Procedure 29, the motion asks the judge to acquit the defendant because the prosecution's evidence is insufficient to sustain a conviction. This motion may also be made after the conclusion of testimony by the defense witnesses. These motions are almost always denied because the prosecution's case is rarely that weak. But if the motion is granted, the defendant goes free; the prosecution cannot appeal such a ruling and the defendant cannot be tried again in federal court on the same charges because of the constitutional protection against double jeopardy. If, however, the judge waits to rule on the motion until after the jury reaches a verdict, and that verdict is guilty, prosecutors can then appeal the judge's acquittal.

> The defendant has the choice whether to testify. No inference of guilt may be drawn by the jurors if the defendant chooses not to testify.

During testimony, both sides will seek to introduce pieces of evidence. If the judge allows an item to be admitted, it becomes part of the public record of the case and should be available for members of the media to inspect and copy. However, your interest in seeing the item sometimes conflicts with the court's interest in insuring none of the evidence is tampered with. This is another of those issues you'll want to broach with your contact person in the clerk's office. Getting a copy of the exhibit from the party that introduced it is another option you can pursue.

Transcripts of courtroom proceedings are provided to the court and litigants by a court reporter. Many court reporters are trained in what is called real-time court reporting, which makes a daily copy of a transcript available, for a fee. As mentioned previously (see the Broadcasting the Trial section), many courts make digital audio recordings of court proceedings publicly available via the PACER service.

Closing Arguments

The prosecution goes first, followed by the defense and a rebuttal by the prosecution. Because the prosecution has the burden of proof, it gets the final word.

Jury Instructions, Deliberations, and the Verdict

After the closing arguments, the judge will give the jury its final instructions. Both sides may contest the content of those instructions because they can have an enormous effect on the jury's verdict.

During deliberations, the jurors may have questions about the evidence or the instructions. They will give a note to the Deputy Marshal or some court employee, who will take it to the judge. The judge will then call the lawyers back into court, discuss what the answer to the note should be, call the jurors back into the courtroom, and give them the answer.

> After a mistrial, prosecutors may retry the defendant on the same charges without violating the Constitution's ban on double jeapordy.

Criminal juries must reach a unanimous verdict of guilty or not guilty. The jury may say at some point that it is hopelessly deadlocked. At this point, judges typically give the jury what's known as an Allen charge. Named after a 1896 U.S. Supreme Court case, the Allen charge urges jurors to reconsider their opinions and try again to reach a verdict. If they attempt to do so but still report they are deadlocked, the judge may declare a mistrial.

In most federal courthouses, once a jury has reached a verdict, it is announced as soon as all the lawyers can get to the courtroom. You may have as little as 15 minutes warning.

Once a jury's members have been dismissed by the judge, you are free to speak to them. (The clerk's office may be willing to provide the names and addresses of the jurors, unless the jury is anonymous.) Still, no juror is obligated to speak with you.

In high-profile cases, the crush of media attention can be overwhelming for some jurors. In such cases judges will sometimes have court security personnel escort the jurors out a back door of the courthouse. You may want to suggest to your contact person in the clerk's office that the judge ask any jurors who would be willing to speak to the media to remain in the jury room or convene at a specific location inside or outside the courthouse. That gives journalists the access they want, while providing a controlled environment in which the jurors can feel comfortable.

Death Penalty Cases

Federal judges, following the U.S. Sentencing Guidelines, determine and impose sentences in all cases except death penalty cases. If a defendant facing the death penalty is found guilty, the same jury that convicted him will determine his sentence. It has only two choices: execution or life in prison. A second phase of the trial, referred to as the penalty phase, then takes place. Both sides can present witnesses who will testify about the seriousness of the crime and any mitigating factors, such as the defendant's life experiences and lack of a prior criminal history.

A Civil Case

Most of the procedures that govern a criminal case also apply to civil cases. The major differences are described below.

Filing the Complaint

Civil cases do not involve an allegation by the government that an individual or entity violated the criminal laws of the United States. Civil cases begin when a plaintiff – the party seeking relief – files a complaint. Federal courts are authorized to hear only civil cases that:

- Deal with a question involving the United States Constitution.
- Involve questions of federal law (as opposed to state law).
- Involve the government of the United States of America – including its agencies – as a party, whether as a plaintiff or defendant.
- Involve a dispute among residents of different states with an amount in controversy more than $75,000.

The act of informing individuals or businesses about a complaint filed against them is called **service of process**.

Generally, a lawsuit must be filed in the jurisdiction where the defendant resides or where the claim arose. In cases based on diversity of citizenship (when the plaintiff and defendant are residents of different states), the lawsuit may be filed in the jurisdiction where the plaintiff resides.

The complaint states the claim that the plaintiff is making – why he, she, or it is entitled to relief. And it states the kind of relief sought. There are three principal forms of relief:

- **Declaratory judgment**: a decision of the court that determines the rights of parties without ordering anything be done or awarding monetary damages.

- **Injunction**: a court order requiring the defendant to do a specific act or prohibiting a defendant from doing a specific act. If a true emergency exists, a **temporary restraining order** can be issued without even providing notice of the lawsuit to the defendant; a TRO can last no more than 10 days. A **preliminary injunction** is similar to a TRO, except that the defendant must receive notice of the lawsuit before the preliminary injunction is issued. The preliminary injunction (sometimes informally referred to as a temporary injunction) stays in effect until a hearing can be held, or sometimes until after a trial. If the plaintiff is successful at trial, a **permanent injunction** would be issued.
- **Monetary relief**: money damages meant to make the plaintiff "whole" for the wrongdoing of the defendant. The two most common types of monetary relief are compensatory and punitive damages. **Compensatory damages** are intended to compensate the injured party for his or her loss. **Special damages** are a subset of compensatory damages; they represent the direct costs of the wrongdoing, such as hospital bills or wages lost while being treated. **General damages** are also a result of the wrongdoing, but are subjective in amount, such as awards for the plaintiff's pain and suffering or a payment for his or her mental anguish. Some contracts anticipate a breach of the agreement and stipulate how much will be awarded in the event a party reneges on the deal; these are called **liquidated damages**. There are also cases where a wrong was committed by the defendant, but the plaintiff suffered almost no harm; **nominal damages**, such as an award of $1, are made in such cases. **Punitive damages**, which generally are available only if authorized by statute, are awarded to punish the defendant and are a warning to others who would consider undertaking similar conduct. **Treble damages** are a variation of punitive damages – triple the amount of the plaintiff's actual losses.

The Defendant's Answer

Under federal rules, defendants generally have 20 days to file an answer after they are served with the complaint; the government of the United States has 60 days. Defendants in cases seeking review of decisions under the Social Security Act have 90 days to answer. Defendants in cases brought under the Freedom of Information Act have 30 days to answer. The complaint and answer should be available for you to see and copy in the clerk's office. In many courts, this information also will be available online.

Motions against the Complaint

Although most defenses to a complaint must be stated in the answer, a defendant has the option of asserting certain defenses in the form of a motion to dismiss the complaint before filing the answer.

Motions to dismiss the complaint typically make one or more of the following arguments:

- The court lacks the power to decide the subject matter of the case or to compel a defendant to appear.
- Service of process was defective.
- The complaint fails to state a claim that the law will recognize as enforceable.

Pretrial Conferences and Hearings

Once the defendant has filed his or her answer or motion to dismiss the complaint, the judge assigned the case will hold a pretrial conference. The conference typically lasts less than an hour. A schedule for discovery – the exchange of information between opposing parties – is generally set at this conference, and a trial date is sometimes also scheduled at this point.

Most motions filed in civil cases involve disputes about whether a party is entitled to receive certain kinds of information prior to trial. While these motions are a part of the case file, the actual information in dispute is almost never filed with the court. During discovery, the parties may take numerous depositions of people involved in the dispute. In a deposition, the witness is under oath and asked questions by the attorneys for both sides, much as they would be if they were on the witness stand in court. This testimony sometimes may be introduced during the trial. Journalists do not have a right to attend depositions in civil cases, as they are not conducted in open court or in the presence of a judge.

When either party files a pretrial motion, the judge may choose to hold a hearing. However, if the judge believes the motion papers are sufficiently clear that the issue can be decided without an oral presentation, no hearing will be held.

After discovery, the judge will hold a final pretrial hearing. Usually, the hearing is a conference between the judge and the parties to discuss the issues that will be tried and the evidence that is to be used at trial. The judge also will usually require that a pretrial order be submitted by the parties, in which the trial plans of the parties are set forth in writing. The purpose is to help the judge and the parties understand exactly what issues will be important at the trial, and to work out possible solutions to problems before the trial begins. Parties frequently discuss settling their case during this final pretrial phase, and it is not uncommon for judges to strongly encourage them to resolve the dispute before trial.

Ending the Case without a Trial

A trial is necessary only when there are disputed issues of fact. After the discovery period has ended, it may become apparent that the facts in the case are not in dispute, and one or more parties may file a motion for summary judgment. A motion for summary judgment can be filed at any time after the answer is filed.

After the motion for summary judgment and the response have been filed, the judge, generally without conducting a hearing, will decide whether or not to grant the motion. If the judge grants the motion in whole, the case will be over and judgment will be entered in favor of the party who moved for summary judgment. If the judge grants the motion in part, only the issues that are in dispute will be tried, and those issues on which summary judgment was granted will not be. If the judge denies the motion, the case will be set for trial. The parties also may resolve their dispute by settlement, without court intervention. The overwhelming majority of civil cases are settled prior to trial.

The Trial

Both the plaintiff and the defendant have the constitutional right to a jury trial. The jury in a civil case consists of no fewer than six and no more than 12 members, not including alternate jurors. All verdicts must be unanimous, unless the parties agree otherwise – an option not available in criminal cases. The plaintiff's lawyer goes first in opening statements, followed by defense counsel, and the plaintiff's witnesses appear first.

Once the plaintiff's last witness has testified, the defendant may, but is not required to, make a motion for a "directed verdict," which is similar to a Rule 29 motion in a criminal case. This motion claims that the plaintiff has failed to prove one or more of the essential elements of the claim for relief and therefore the defendant is entitled to judgment in his favor as a matter of law.

Unlike criminal juries, which can only find a defendant guilty if the evidence is beyond a reasonable doubt, civil juries find the facts based on the preponderance of the evidence standard – that is, it is more likely than not that factual issues supporting the plaintiff's claims have been proven to be true.

Courtroom Equipment

Advances in courtroom technologies can both streamline litigation and increase juror understanding. For the federal judiciary, the modern courtroom offers four basic features:

- An **evidence presentation system** that enables the judge or lawyers to show jurors and each other case documents and exhibits on a network of monitors. Large courtroom monitors allow the public to follow the proceedings.
- **Video-teleconferencing**, which, among other things, permits offsite witnesses to offer “live” testimony during trial and accommodates appellate proceedings without all participating judges and lawyers being physically present.
- **Integrated CD-ROM, video and audio capability**, which allows lawyers to present their cases on videotape, audiotape, or through CD-ROM players attached to personal computers.
- **Realtime transcription**, a system that allows a court reporter's transcription to be viewed virtually simultaneously on monitors placed throughout the courtroom for use by the judge, lawyers, and jurors.

BANKRUPTCY COURT

Federal courts have exclusive jurisdiction over bankruptcy cases. The primary purposes of the federal bankruptcy laws are to give an honest debtor, either a person or a business, a “fresh start” in life by relieving the debtor of most debts, and to repay creditors in an orderly manner to the extent that the debtor has property available for payment. That can be done using several different methods, as identified by chapter numbers of the U.S. Bankruptcy Code, Title 11 of the United States Code.

There are 90 U.S. bankruptcy courts, which, by statute, are units of the U.S. district courts. A U.S. bankruptcy judge presides over a bankruptcy case. The judge is appointed to a 14-year term by the judges of the local U.S. Court of Appeals and can be reappointed. Like district courts, bankruptcy courts have their own local rules. Each court's local rules are available at the court's web site, all of which can be accessed at http://www.uscourts.gov. A publication, "Bankruptcy Basics," offers a good explanation of bankruptcy law and bankruptcy court proceedings. It is available online at http://www.uscourts.gov/FederalCourts/Bankruptcy/ BankruptcyBasics.aspx.

Bankruptcy court proceedings are open to the public and the news media unless some extraordinary circumstance exists, such as the judge considering a matter under seal. As in other federal courts, all bankruptcy proceedings are recorded. Bankruptcy judges are authorized to use either contract court reporters (not employees of the court) or electronic sound recording equipment. You may order a transcript of a bankruptcy proceeding through the contract court reporter or through a professional transcription service chosen by the court.

All documents filed in connection with a bankruptcy case generally are considered public documents and can be viewed at the court clerk's office or through the court's PACER system (see www.pacer.gov).

Bankruptcy courts generally have their own clerks, but in some judicial districts the clerk's operations of the district and bankruptcy courts are consolidated.

Bankruptcy generally provides two options: liquidation or reorganization. Liquidation means selling off a debtor's assets, if there are any available, to raise cash for creditors. Chapter 7 of the Bankruptcy Code is designed for that purpose. When a Chapter 7 case is filed, a trustee is appointed by the United States Trustee to take over the debtor's property for the benefit of creditors. A debtor who is an individual, however, is allowed to keep a limited amount of "exempt" property specified by law. The great majority of cases filed under Chapter 7, however, are "no assets" cases, in which the debtor has not assets available for distribution to creditors.

Reorganization involves obtaining a bankruptcy judge's approval of a plan for repayment over time of all or a percentage of the debts owed to creditors. Chapters 11 and 13 govern the reorganization of a debtor's financial affairs. Chapter 13 cases involve obtaining a bankruptcy judge's approval of a plan for repayment over time of all or a percentage of the debts owed to creditors. Chapter 11 cases, nearly always filed by corporations or other business entities, involve a plan of reorganization of the debtor's liabilities, which must be voted on by creditors and approved by a bankruptcy judge.

In all cases, no matter what chapter, a "meeting of creditors" must be held, usually from 20 to 40 days after a bankruptcy petition is filed. The debtor must attend this meeting, at which creditors may ask questions regarding the debtor's financial affairs and the extent of the debtor's holdings. A trustee, not a bankruptcy judge, presides over this hearing.

There are several types of bankruptcy proceedings that may interest journalists. The first is a hearing on **first day orders**, which are sometimes held in Chapter 11 cases. At this hearing, a bankruptcy judge is asked to approve important matters that determine how the debtor will operate while the case is pending. Another hearing in a Chapter 11 case is held for **confirmation of the debtor's plan of reorganization**. During this hearing, the debtor's lawyer attempts to obtain the judge's approval of the plan, and creditors have a chance to present their objections to the plan.

Still another proceeding of interest is an adversary hearing – something of a mini-trial involving a particular issue related to the main bankruptcy case. Adversary proceedings can focus, among other things, on requests for injunctions, environmental issues, and fraud on the part of the debtor.

Appeals of a bankruptcy judge's rulings can be made to the district court, or, in certain circuits, to a bankruptcy appellate panel composed of three bankruptcy judges. Further appeals to the court of appeals and the Supreme Court are then available. If certain statutory requirements are met, the court of appeals also has jurisdiction to authorize a direct appeal from a bankruptcy judge's ruling to the court of appeals.

Bankruptcy court records are available online through the PACER system (www.pacer.gov) or through each court's web site, accessible through http://www.uscourts.gov. The court web sites also contain local rules, practice preferences of individual judges, and other useful information.

COVERING FEDERAL APPELLATE COURT

The nation's 94 federal judicial districts are organized into 12 regional circuits, each of which has a United States court of appeals. A court of appeals hears appeals from the district courts located within its circuit, as well as appeals from decisions of federal administrative agencies and some original proceedings filed directly with the courts of appeals.

A list of the 12 regional circuits and of the judicial districts they encompass is in the appendix.

The Court of Appeals for the Federal Circuit is based in Washington, D.C., and has nationwide jurisdiction to hear appeals in specialized cases. The court hears appeals from the U.S. Court of International Trade, the U.S. Court of Federal Claims, and the U.S. Patent and Trademark Office. It also exclusively hears certain types of cases appealed from the district courts, primarily those involving patent laws.

The Appeals Process

The losing party in a decision by a federal trial court usually has the right to appeal the final decision to a federal court of appeals. Similarly, a litigant not satisfied with a decision made by a federal administrative agency usually may seek review by a court of appeals. Parties who contest decisions made in certain federal agencies – for example, disputes over Social Security benefits – may be required to seek review first in a district court rather than go directly to an appeals court.

In a civil case, either side may appeal the judgment based on a jury verdict or bench trial. In a criminal case, the defendant may appeal a conviction based on a guilty verdict, but the government may not appeal if a defendant is found not guilty. Either side in a criminal case may appeal a sentence that is imposed after a guilty verdict if it departs from the sentencing guidelines.

If the dissatisfied party in the district court plans an appeal, the first step usually is to file a **notice of appeal** in the district court, which informs the court of appeals and other parties.

A litigant who files an appeal from a district court decision is known as an **appellant**. The term "petitioner" is used for a litigant who files an appeal from an administrative agency or who appeals an original proceeding. The appellant (petitioner) bears the burden of showing that the trial court or administrative agency made a legal error that affected the decision in the case.

The court of appeals makes its decision based on the record of the case established by the trial court or agency. The court of appeals does not receive additional evidence or hear witnesses. The court of appeals also may review the factual findings made by the trial court or agency, but typically may overturn a decision on factual grounds only if the findings were "clearly erroneous."

Three-Judge Panels

Appeals normally are decided by panels of three judges working together. A panel may include a senior circuit or district judge, a district judge from a district court within the particular circuit, or a visiting circuit or district judge from another circuit. In general, judges are assigned to panels randomly. The judges may play no role in determining who will sit on which panel or in the assignment of cases to a particular panel. Indeed, the creation of the panels and the assignment of cases to individual panels are separate functions often performed by different court units.

Additionally, judges do not participate in cases in which their participation would constitute a conflict of interest or create an appearance of impropriety. In such circumstances, the judge should recuse himself or herself from the case.

The appellant presents legal arguments to the panel in a written brief, seeking to persuade the judges that the trial court committed substantial error, and that the trial court's decision should therefore be reversed. The party who prevailed in the trial court, known as the **appellee** (or **respondent** for administrative agency appeals), argues in a reply brief that the trial court was correct, or that any error made was not significant enough to affect the outcome of the case.

In the majority of circuits, most appeals are decided solely on the basis of briefs submitted to the court. In other circuits, the court more often renders its decision after **oral argument**, which is a structured discussion in which both sides present arguments on the legal principles in the dispute. Each side is given a short time, typically 15 minutes, to present its case, but the judges may interrupt to ask any questions they have. Oral arguments traditionally are open to the public.

Judicial Conference policy leaves it to the individual appellate courts to decide whether electronic and photographic coverage of oral arguments will be allowed. The Second and Ninth Circuits will consider requests for such coverage in civil cases. The Seventh, Eighth and Ninth Circuits make available on the Internet digital recordings of oral arguments.

Some time after the submission of briefs or after oral argument, the court of appeals will issue a decision, usually accompanied by an opinion explaining its rationale. A decision may be reached by a 3-0 or 2-1 vote. A decision will take into account and apply any relevant **precedents**, similar cases already decided by that court, or by the Supreme Court.

This decision will be controlling unless: (1) the judges send the case back to the trial court for additional proceedings (i.e. remand the case); (2) the court determines on its own that the matter should be reheard because of a potential conflict with a prior decision; (3) the parties seek a rehearing before the panel; (4) the parties seek review before the full appeals court (called an *en banc* session); or (5) the parties seek review in the U.S. Supreme Court.

Federal courts of appeals issue tens of thousands of decisions each year, and only a small percentage of them are taken to the Supreme Court, which grants review only to a fraction of the cases it receives. Opinions issued by the courts of appeals and by the Supreme Court are posted on the respective court web sites.

Bankruptcy Appellate Panels

Appeals of decisions made by bankruptcy judges may be filed with the district court, or, in some circuits, with the bankruptcy appellate panel, which is composed of three bankruptcy judges from within the circuit. The law requires the judicial council of each circuit to establish a bankruptcy appellate panel to hear bankruptcy appeals unless the **judicial council** (see definition in **Key Players** section below) finds that there are insufficient judicial resources in the circuit, or that the establishment of a bankruptcy appellate panel would result in undue delay or increased costs to the parties in bankruptcy cases.

There are two additional requirements that must be satisfied before an appeal in a bankruptcy case can be heard by a bankruptcy appellate panel: the district judges in each district must authorize the referral of appeals from the district court to the bankruptcy appellate panel; and the parties to the appeal must consent to the appeal being heard by the panel. A member of the bankruptcy appellant panel may not hear an appeal originating in the district from which such member is appointed. Whether an appeal is heard by a district judge or a bankruptcy appellate panel, any further appeal of a bankruptcy case must be made to the court of appeals.

A bankruptcy appellate panel has been established in the First, Sixth, Eighth, Ninth, and Tenth Circuits. In the First, Ninth, and Tenth Circuits, the panels may hear bankruptcy appeals from all districts in their circuits. The Sixth Circuit panel may hear bankruptcy appeals from all districts in the circuit except those arising from the Western District of Kentucky, the Eastern District of Michigan, and the Eastern District of Tennessee. The Eighth Circuit panel may hear all bankruptcy appeals in the circuit except those arising from the District of South Dakota.

Key Players

Federal court of appeals judges are Article III judges appointed for life. Each judge is authorized to maintain a staff that usually includes three law clerks and two secretaries (judicial assistants).

The **chief judge** has an important role in court management. By statute, the chief judge is the judge senior in commission who, at the inception of chief judge service, has served on the court at least one year and is under the age of 65. A chief judge may serve for a maximum of seven years, and may not serve as chief judge beyond the age of 70. As the presiding official of a court of appeals, the chief judge has both legal and functional authority over court administration.

The chief judge has specific statutory responsibilities for the management of the court and its cases, to facilitate the smooth and efficient operation of the court and the timely hearing and disposition of cases. For example, the chief judge has responsibility to ensure the administration of cases by providing a sufficient number of judges to sit on appellate panels. This includes the authority to certify the need for a temporary assignment of a judge from another circuit to serve on a district court or the court of appeals; to designate or assign a circuit judge with the circuit to hold district court in any district within the circuit; to designate or assign a district judge to sit on the court of appeals; or to designate or assign temporarily a district judge to hold a district court in any district in the circuit. The chief judge has statutory authority to certify that an emergency exists that would permit the formation of a panel not consisting of a majority of judges from the same court of appeals, which normally is required by statute.

The chief judge also has administrative responsibilities relating to the court's operation, including presiding over court meetings and coordinating decision-making activities of the court. This includes the appointment and oversight of a court staff, including the clerk of court and the senior staff attorney. The chief judge's responsibilities include budgetary and administrative authority.

The chief judge also presides over the **circuit judicial council**, which is vested with authority to "make all necessary and appropriate orders for the effective and expeditious administration of justice within its circuit." (28 U.S.C. Section 332(d)(1)). In addition to the chief judge, the council consists of an equal number of appellate and district judges. The Judicial Conference has called on judicial councils to take on more specific responsibilities, such as approving temporary emergency support for chambers within each circuit.

Each circuit has a **circuit executive** who works closely with the chief judge to coordinate a wide range of administrative matters. The circuit executive is appointed by the circuit judicial council. Each court of appeals also is organized into the following court units: clerk's office, staff attorney office, circuit mediation office, and, in some circuits, clerk for the bankruptcy appellate panel.

In some circuits, the circuit executive serves as a liaison between the court and the news media. In other circuits, however, that responsibility may belong to the appeals court's **clerk of court**, whose staff manages the flow of cases through the court, maintains court records, and handles other administrative duties. The clerk of court is responsible for central records keeping, maintaining caseload statistics, and maintaining automation (information technology) systems necessary for the effective operation of the court.

Another member of a court of appeals' management team may be its **senior staff attorney**, who supervises an office of attorneys whose duties range from reviewing all appeals filed by prison inmates without a lawyer's help to drafting proposed opinions on preliminary matters.

Each court of appeals has a circuit mediation program, also referred to as a conference attorney program. Although programs vary from court to court, the primary goal of the program is to achieve settlement of pending cases prior to submission to a panel of judges for decision.

The circuit librarian is appointed by each court of appeals and is responsible for the administration of the library program and related services within the circuit.

An important inquiry early on in any journalist's dealings with a federal court of appeals is to identify the person(s) within the court authorized to talk to the news media. Most courts of appeals do not have a public information officer, but the circuit executive or clerk of court likely has designated an individual who deals with the news media on a daily basis.

Types and Sources of Court Information

Federal appeals courts comply with the Federal Rules of Appellate Procedure, which can be found online, at http://www.uscourts.gov/uscourts/RulesAndPolicies/rules/AP2009.pdf In addition, each appeals court has its own local rules, which are posted on its web site. A court's rules govern the various deadlines imposed on all parties in a case, and dictate the pace of a case, from initial filing to resolution.

You can visit an appeals court's web site by going to the Judiciary's web site, www. uscourts.gov, and clicking on Court Locator. Decisions, opinions, orders, and court calendars may be found on the court's web site.

The clerk's office maintains court records, including briefs filed in appellate cases, as well as court calendars and other information provided to the public.

On occasion, a lone appellate judge will handle an emergency matter. The papers filed in such a case and the order issued by the judge will be on file in the clerk's office, and they also may be posted on the court's web site.

GLOSSARY

a

Acquittal – A jury verdict that a criminal defendant is not guilty, or the finding of a judge that the evidence is insufficient to support a conviction.

Active Judge – A judge in the full-time service of the court. Compare to senior judge.

Administrative Office of the United States Courts (AO) – The federal agency responsible for collecting court statistics, administering the federal courts' budget, and performing many other administrative and programmatic functions, under the direction and supervision of the Judicial Conference of the United States.

Admissible – A term used to describe evidence that may be considered by a jury or judge in civil and criminal cases.

Affidavit – A written or printed statement made under oath.

Alternate Juror – A juror selected in the same manner as a regular juror who hears all the evidence but does not help decide the case unless called on to replace a regular juror.

Alternative Dispute Resolution (ADR) – A procedure for settling a dispute outside the courtroom. Most forms of ADR are not binding on the parties, and involve referral of the case to a neutral party such as an arbitrator or mediator.

Amicus Curiae – Latin for "friend of the court." It is advice formally offered to the court in a brief filed by an entity interested in, but not a party to, the case.

Answer – The formal written statement by a defendant in a civil case that responds to a complaint, articulating the grounds for defense.

Appellant – The party who appeals a district court's decision, usually seeking reversal of that decision.

Appellee – The party who opposes an appellant's appeal, and who seeks to persuade the appeals court to affirm the district court's decision.

Arraignment – A proceeding in which a criminal defendant is brought into court, told of the charges in an indictment or information, and asked to plead guilty or not guilty.

Article III Judge – A federal judge who is appointed for life, during "good behavior," under Article III of the Constitution. Article III judges are nominated by the President and confirmed by the Senate.

b

Bail – The release, prior to trial, of a person accused of a crime, under specified conditions designed to assure that person's appearance in court when required. Also can refer to the amount of bond money posted as a financial condition of pretrial release.

Bankruptcy Judge – A judicial officer of the United States district court who is the court official with decision-making power over federal bankruptcy cases.

Bench Trial – A trial without a jury, in which the judge serves as the fact-finder.

Brief – A written statement submitted in a trial or appellate proceeding that explains one side's legal and factual arguments.

Burden of Proof – The duty to prove disputed facts. In civil cases, a plaintiff generally has the burden of proving his or her case. In criminal cases, the government has the burden of proving the defendant's guilt. (See standard of proof.)

c

Case File – A complete collection of every document filed in court in a case.

Case Law – The law as established in previous court decisions. A synonym for legal precedent. Akin to common law, which springs from tradition and judicial decisions.

Caseload – The number of cases handled by a judge or a court.

Cause of Action – A legal claim.

Chambers – The offices of a judge and his or her staff.

Class Action – A lawsuit in which one or more members of a large group, or class, of individuals or other entities sue on behalf of the entire class. The district court must find that the claims of the class members contain questions of law or fact in common before the lawsuit can proceed as a class action.

Clerk of Court – The court officer who oversees administrative functions, especially managing the flow of cases through the court. The clerk's office is often called a court's central nervous system.

Complaint – A written statement that begins a civil lawsuit, in which the plaintiff details the claims against the defendant.

Concurrent Sentence – Prison terms for two or more offenses to be served at the same time, rather than one after the other. Example: Two five-year sentences and one three-year sentence, if served concurrently, result in a maximum of five years behind bars.

Consecutive Sentence – Prison terms for two or more offenses to be served one after the other. Example: Two five-year sentences and one three-year sentence, if served consecutively, result in a maximum of 13 years behind bars.

Count – An allegation in an indictment or information, charging a defendant with a crime. An indictment or information may contain allegations that the defendant committed more than one crime. Each allegation is referred to as a count.

d

Damages – Money that a defendant pays a plaintiff in a civil case if the plaintiff has won. Damages may be compensatory (for loss or injury) or punitive (to punish and deter future misconduct).

Declaratory Judgment – A judge's statement about someone's rights. For example, a plaintiff may seek a declaratory judgment that a particular statute, as written, violates some constitutional right.

De Facto – Latin, meaning "in fact" or "actually." Something that exists in fact but not as a matter of law.

Default Judgment – A judgment awarding a plaintiff the relief sought in the complaint because the defendant has failed to appear in court or otherwise respond to the complaint.

De Jure – Latin, meaning "in law." Something that exists by operation of law.

De Novo – Latin, meaning "anew." A trial de novo is a completely new trial. Appellate review de novo implies no deference to the trial judge's ruling.

Discharge – A release of a debtor from personal liability for certain debts, preventing creditors from taking any action against the debtor or the debtor's property to collect the debts.

Discovery – Procedures used to obtain disclosure of evidence before trial.

Dismissal with Prejudice – Court action that prevents an identical lawsuit from being filed later.

Dismissal without Prejudice – Court action that allows the later filing.

Due Process – In criminal law, the constitutional guarantee that a defendant will receive a fair and impartial trial. In civil law, the legal rights of someone who confronts an adverse action threatening liberty or property.

e

En Banc – French, meaning "on the bench." All judges of an appellate court sitting together to hear a case, as opposed to the routine disposition by panels of three judges. In the Ninth Circuit, an en banc panel consists of 11 randomly selected judges.

Exclusionary Rule – Doctrine that says evidence obtained in violation of a criminal defendant's constitutional or statutory rights is not admissible at trial.

Exculpatory Evidence – Evidence indicating that a defendant did not commit the crime.

Ex Parte – A proceeding brought before a court by one party only, without notice to or challenge by the other side.

f

Federal Public Defender Organization – As provided for in the Criminal Justice Act, an organization established within a federal judicial circuit to represent criminal defendants who cannot afford an adequate defense. Each organization is supervised by a federal public defender appointed by the court of appeals for the circuit.

Felony – A serious crime, usually punishable by at least one year in prison.

h

Habeas Corpus – Latin, meaning "you have the body." A writ of habeas corpus generally is a judicial order forcing law enforcement authorities to produce a prisoner they are holding, and to justify the prisoner's continued confinement. Federal judges receive petitions for a writ of habeas corpus from state prison inmates who say their state prosecutions violated federally protected rights in some way.

Hearsay – Evidence presented by a witness who did not see or hear the incident in question but heard about it from someone else. With some exceptions, hearsay generally is not admissible as evidence at trial.

i

In Camera – Latin, meaning in a judge's chambers. Often means outside the presence of a jury and the public. In private.

Inculpatory Evidence – Evidence indicating that a defendant did commit the crime.

Injunction – A court order preventing one or more named parties from taking some action. A preliminary injunction often is issued to allow fact-finding, so a judge can determine whether a permanent injunction is justified.

Interrogatories – A form of discovery consisting of written questions to be answered in writing and under oath.

j

Judicial Conference of the United States – The policy-making entity for the federal court system. A 27-judge body whose presiding officer is the Chief Justice of the United States.

Jurisdiction – The legal authority of a court to hear and decide a certain type of case. It also is used as a synonym for venue, meaning the geographic area over which the court has territorial jurisdiction to decide cases.

m

Moot – Not subject to a court ruling because the controversy has not actually arisen, or has ended.

Motion in Limine – A pretrial motion requesting the court to prohibit the other side from presenting, or even referring to, evidence on matters said to be so highly prejudicial that no steps taken by the judge can prevent the jury from being unduly influenced.

p

Per Curiam – Latin, meaning "for the court." In appellate courts, often refers to an unsigned opinion.

Peremptory Challenge – A district court may grant each side in a civil or criminal trial the right to exclude a certain number of prospective jurors without cause or giving a reason.

Probation – An alternative to prison, it is conditional freedom for an offender.

Pro Se – Representing oneself. Serving as one's own lawyer.

Pro Tem – Temporary.

r

Remand – Send back.

s

Sanction – A penalty or other type of enforcement used to bring about compliance with the law or with rules and regulations.

Senior Judge – A federal judge who, after attaining the requisite age and length of judicial experience, takes senior status, thus creating a vacancy among a court's active judges. A senior judge retains the judicial office and may cut back his or her workload by as much as 75 percent, but many opt to keep a larger caseload.

Standard of Proof – Degree of proof required. In criminal cases, prosecutors must prove a defendant's guilt "beyond a reasonable doubt." The majority of civil lawsuits require proof "by a preponderance of the evidence" (50 percent plus), but in some the standard is higher and requires "clear and convincing" proof.

Statute of Limitations – The time within which a lawsuit must be filed or a criminal prosecution begun. The deadline can vary, depending on the type of civil case or the crime charged.

Sua Sponte – Latin, meaning "of its own will." Often refers to a court taking an action in a case without being asked to do so by either side.

Subpoena – A command, issued under a court's authority, to a witness to appear and give testimony.

t

Temporary Restraining Order – Akin to a preliminary injunction, it is a judge's short-term order forbidding certain actions until a full hearing can be conducted. Often referred to as a TRO.

341 Meeting – A meeting of creditors at which the debtor is questioned under oath by creditors, a trustee, examiner, or the United States trustee about his/her financial affairs.

Tort – A civil, not criminal, wrong. A negligent or intentional injury against a person or property, with the exception of breach of contract.

Trustee – The representative of the bankruptcy estate who exercises statutory powers, principally for the benefit of the unsecured creditors, under the general supervision of the court and the direct supervision of the United States trustee or bankruptcy administrator.

V

Venue – The geographic area in which a court has jurisdiction. A **change of venue** is a change or transfer of a case from one judicial district to another.

Voir Dire – Jury selection process of questioning prospective jurors, to ascertain their qualifications and determine any basis for challenge.

W

Warrant – Court authorization, most often for law enforcement officers, to conduct a search or make an arrest.

Writ – A written court order directing a person to take, or refrain from taking, a certain act.

APPENDIX A.

Federal Judiciary Web Sites

Administrative Office and Federal Judicial Center

- Federal Courts Home Page - http://www.uscourts.gov/FederalCourts
- Federal Judicial Center - http://www.fjc.gov/
- PACER Service Center - http://www.pacer.gov
- PACER Case Locator - http://www.pacer.gov/pcl.html

1st Circuit

- Court of Appeals - http://www.ca1.uscourts.gov/
- Maine Bankruptcy Court - http://www.meb.uscourts.gov/
- Maine District Court - http://www.med.uscourts.gov/
- Massachusetts Bankruptcy Court - http://www.mab.uscourts.gov/
- Massachusetts District Court - http://www.mad.uscourts.gov/
- New Hampshire Bankruptcy Court - http://www.nhb.uscourts.gov/
- New Hampshire District Court - http://www.nhd.uscourts.gov/
- Puerto Rico Bankruptcy Court - http://www.prb.uscourts.gov/
- Puerto Rico District Court - http://www.prd.uscourts.gov/
- Puerto Rico Pretrial Services Office - http://www.prpt.uscourts.gov/
- Puerto Rico Probation Office - http://www.prp.uscourts.gov/

- Rhode Island Bankruptcy Court - http://www.rib.uscourts.gov/
- Rhode Island District Court - http://www.rid.uscourts.gov/

2nd Circuit

- Connecticut Bankruptcy Court - http://www.ctb.uscourts.gov/
- Connecticut District Court - http://www.ctd.uscourts.gov/
- Court of Appeals - http://www.ca2.uscourts.gov/
- New York Eastern Bankruptcy Court - http://www.nyeb.uscourts.gov/
- New York Eastern District Court - http://www.nyed.uscourts.gov/
- New York Northern Bankruptcy Court - http://www.nynb.uscourts.gov/
- New York Northern District Court - http://www.nynd.uscourts.gov/
- New York Southern Bankruptcy Court - http://www.nysb.uscourts.gov/
- New York Southern District Court - http://www.nysd.uscourts.gov/
- New York Western Bankruptcy Court - http://www.nywb.uscourts.gov/
- New York Western District Court - http://www.nywd.uscourts.gov/
- Vermont Bankruptcy Court - http://www.vtb.uscourts.gov/
- Vermont District Court - http://www.vtd.uscourts.gov/

3rd Circuit

- Court of Appeals - http://www.ca3.uscourts.gov/
- Delaware Bankruptcy Court - http://www.deb.uscourts.gov/
- Delaware District Court - http://www.ded.uscourts.gov/
- New Jersey Bankruptcy Court - http://www.njb.uscourts.gov/
- New Jersey District Court - http://pacer.njd.uscourts.gov/
- New Jersey Pretrial Services - http://www.njpt.uscourts.gov/
- Pennsylvania Eastern Bankruptcy Court - http://www.paeb.uscourts.gov/
- Pennsylvania Eastern District Court - http://www.paed.uscourts.gov/
- Pennsylvania Middle Bankruptcy Court - http://www.pamb.uscourts.gov/
- Pennsylvania Middle District Court - http://www.pamd.uscourts.gov/
- Pennsylvania Western Bankruptcy Court - http://www.pawb.uscourts.gov/
- Pennsylvania Western District Court - http://www.pawd.uscourts.gov/
- Virgin Islands District Court - http://www.vid.uscourts.gov/

4th Circuit

- Court of Appeals - http://www.ca4.uscourts.gov/
- Maryland Bankruptcy Court - http://www.mdb.uscourts.gov
- Maryland District Court - http://www.mdd.uscourts.gov/
- North Carolina Eastern Bankruptcy Court - http://www.nceb.uscourts.gov/
- North Carolina Eastern District Court - http://www.nced.uscourts.gov/
- North Carolina Middle Bankruptcy Court - http://www.ncmb.uscourts.gov/
- North Carolina Middle District Court - http://www.ncmd.uscourts.gov/
- North Carolina Western Bankruptcy Court - http://www.ncwb.uscourts.gov/
- North Carolina Western District Court - http://www.ncwd.uscourts.gov/
- South Carolina Bankruptcy Court - http://www.scb.uscourts.gov/
- South Carolina District Court - http://www.scd.uscourts.gov/
- Virginia Eastern Bankruptcy Court - http://www.vaeb.uscourts.gov/
- Virginia Eastern District Court - http://www.vaed.uscourts.gov/
- Virginia Eastern Pretrial Services Office - http://www.vaept.uscourts.gov/
- Virginia Western Bankruptcy Court - http://www.vawb.uscourts.gov/
- Virginia Western District Court - http://www.vawd.uscourts.gov/
- West Virginia Northern Bankruptcy Court - http://www.wvnb.uscourts.gov/
- West Virginia Northern District Court - http://www.wvnd.uscourts.gov/
- West Virginia Southern Bankruptcy Court - http://www.wvsb.uscourts.gov/
- West Virginia Southern District Court - http://www.wvsd.uscourts.gov/
- West Virginia Southern Probation Office - http://www.wvsd.uscourts.gov/probation/default.html

5th Circuit

- Court of Appeals - http://www.ca5.uscourts.gov/
- Louisiana Eastern Bankruptcy Court - http://www.laeb.uscourts.gov/
- Louisiana Eastern District Court - http://www.laed.uscourts.gov/

- Louisiana Eastern Pretrial Services Office - http://www.laed.uscourts.gov/directories/ pretrial.htm
- Louisiana Eastern District Probation Office - http://www.laed.uscourts.gov/directories/probation.htm
- Louisiana Middle Bankruptcy Court - http://www.lamb.uscourts.gov/
- Louisiana Middle District Court - http://www.lamd.uscourts.gov/
- Louisiana Western Bankruptcy Court - http://www.lawb.uscourts.gov/
- Louisiana Western District Court - http://www.lawd.uscourts.gov/
- Mississippi Northern Bankruptcy Court - http://www.msnb.uscourts.gov/
- Mississippi Northern District Court - http://www.msnd.uscourts.gov/
- Mississippi Southern Bankruptcy Court - http://www.mssb.uscourts.gov/
- Mississippi Southern District Court - http://www.mssd.uscourts.gov/
- Texas Eastern Bankruptcy Court - http://www.txeb.uscourts.gov/
- Texas Eastern District Court - http://www.txed.uscourts.gov/
- Texas Eastern Probation Office - http://www.txep.uscourts.gov/
- Texas Northern Bankruptcy Court - http://www.txnb.uscourts.gov/
- Texas Northern District Court - http://www.txnd.uscourts.gov/
- Texas Southern District/Bankruptcy Courts - http://www.txs.uscourts.gov/
- Texas Western Bankruptcy Court - http://www.txwb.uscourts.gov/
- Texas Western District Court - http://www.txwd.uscourts.gov/

6th Circuit

- Court of Appeals - http://www.ca6.uscourts.gov/
- Kentucky Eastern Bankruptcy Court - http://www.kyeb.uscourts.gov/
- Kentucky Eastern District Court - http://www.kyed.uscourts.gov/
- Kentucky Western Bankruptcy Court - http://www.kywb.uscourts.gov/
- Kentucky Western District Court - http://www.kywd.uscourts.gov/
- Kentucky Western Probation Office - http://www.kywp.uscourts.gov/
- Michigan Eastern Bankruptcy Court - http://www.mieb.uscourts.gov/
- Michigan Eastern District - http://www.mied.uscourts.gov/
- Michigan Eastern Probation Office - http://www.mied.uscourts.gov/_probation
- Michigan Western Bankruptcy Court - http://www.miwb.uscourts.gov/

- Michigan Western District Court - http://www.miwd.uscourts.gov/
- Ohio Northern Bankruptcy Court - http://www.ohnb.uscourts.gov/
- Ohio Northern District Court - http://www.ohnd.uscourts.gov/
- Ohio Southern Bankruptcy Court - http://www.ohsb.uscourts.gov/
- Ohio Southern District Court - http://www.ohsd.uscourts.gov/
- Ohio Southern Probation - http://www.ohsp.uscourts.gov/
- Tennessee Eastern Bankruptcy Court - http://www.tneb.uscourts.gov/
- Tennessee Eastern District Court - http://www.tned.uscourts.gov/
- Tennessee Middle Bankruptcy Court - http://www.tnmb.uscourts.gov/
- Tennessee Middle District Court - http://www.tnmd.uscourts.gov/
- Tennessee Middle Probation & Pretrial Services Office - http://www.tnmp. uscourts.gov/
- Tennessee Western Bankruptcy Court - http://www.tnwb.uscourts.gov/
- Tennessee Western District Court - http://www.tnwd.uscourts.gov/
- Tennessee Western Probation Office - http://www.tnwp.uscourts.gov/

7th Circuit

- Court of Appeals - http://www.ca7.uscourts.gov/
- Illinois Central Bankruptcy Court - http://www.ilcb.uscourts.gov/
- Illinois Central District Court - http://www.ilcd.uscourts.gov/
  Illinois Northern Bankruptcy Court - http://www.ilnb.uscourts.gov/
- Illinois Northern District Court - http://www.ilnd.uscourts.gov/
- Illinois Southern Bankruptcy Court - http://www.ilsb.uscourts.gov/
- Illinois Southern District Court - http://www.ilsd.uscourts.gov/
- Illinois Southern Probation Office - http://www.ilsd.uscourts.gov/uspo/default.html
- Indiana Northern Bankruptcy Court - http://www.innb.uscourts.gov/
- Indiana Northern District Court - http://www.innd.uscourts.gov/
- Indiana Northern Probation and Pretrial - http://www.innp.uscourts.gov/
- Indiana Southern Bankruptcy Court - http://www.insb.uscourts.gov/
- Indiana Southern District Court - http://www.insd.uscourts.gov/
- Indiana Southern Probation Office - http://www.insp.uscourts.gov/
- Wisconsin Eastern Bankruptcy Court - http://www.wieb.uscourts.gov/
- Wisconsin Eastern District Court - http://www.wied.uscourts.gov/
- Wisconsin Western Bankruptcy Court - http://www.wiw.uscourts.gov/bankruptcy/

- Wisconsin Western District Court - http://www.wiwd.uscourts.gov/
- Wisconsin Western Probation Office - http://www.wiw.uscourts.gov

8th Circuit

- Arkansas Eastern District Court - http://www.are.uscourts.gov/
- Arkansas Eastern and Western Bankruptcy Court - http://www.arb.uscourts.gov/
- Arkansas Western District Court - http://www.arwd.uscourts.gov/
- Court of Appeals - http://www.ca8.uscourts.gov/
- Iowa Northern Bankruptcy Court - http://www.ianb.uscourts.gov/
- Iowa Northern District Court - http://www.iand.uscourts.gov/
- Iowa Southern Bankruptcy Court - http://www.iasb.uscourts.gov/
- Iowa Southern District Court - http://www.iasd.uscourts.gov/
- Minnesota Bankruptcy Court - http://www.mnb.uscourts.gov/
- Minnesota District Court - http://www.mnd.uscourts.gov/
- Missouri Eastern Bankruptcy Court - http://www.moeb.uscourts.gov/
- Missouri Eastern District Court - http://www.moed.uscourts.gov/
- Missouri Eastern Pretrial Services - http://www.moept.uscourts.gov/
- Missouri Eastern Probation Office - http://www.moep.uscourts.gov/
- Missouri Western District and Bankruptcy Courts - http://www.mow.uscourts.gov/
- Nebraska Bankruptcy Court - http://www.neb.uscourts.gov/
- Nebraska District Court - http://www.ned.uscourts.gov/
- North Dakota Bankruptcy Court - http://www.ndb.uscourts.gov/
- North Dakota District Court - http://www.ndd.uscourts.gov/
- South Dakota Bankruptcy Court - http://www.sdb.uscourts.gov/
- South Dakota District Court - http://www.sdd.uscourts.gov/

9th Circuit

- Alaska Bankruptcy Court - http://www.akb.uscourts.gov/
- Alaska District Court - http://www.akd.uscourts.gov/
- Arizona Bankruptcy Court - http://www.azb.uscourts.gov/
- Arizona District Court - http://www.azd.uscourts.gov/
- Bankruptcy Appellate Panel of the Ninth Circuit - http://www.ce9.uscourts.gov/bap
- California Central Bankruptcy Court - http://www.cacb.uscourts.gov/
- California Central District Court - http://www.cacd.uscourts.gov/
- California Eastern Bankruptcy Court - http://www.caeb.uscourts.gov/

- California Eastern District Court - http://www.caed.uscourts.gov/
- California Eastern Probation Office - http://www.caep.uscourts.gov/
- California Northern Bankruptcy Court - http://www.canb.uscourts.gov/
- California Northern District Court - http://www.cand.uscourts.gov/
- California Southern Bankruptcy Court - http://www.casb.uscourts.gov/
- California Southern District Court - http://www.casd.uscourts.gov/
- California Southern Pretrial Services - http://www.caspt.uscourts.gov/
- California Southern Probation Office - http://www.casp.uscourts.gov/
- Court of Appeals - http://www.ca9.uscourts.gov/
- Guam District Court - http://www.gud.uscourts.gov/
- Hawaii Bankruptcy Court - http://www.hib.uscourts.gov/
- Hawaii District Court - http://www.hid.uscourts.gov/
- Idaho Bankruptcy/District Court - http://www.id.uscourts.gov/
- Montana Bankruptcy Court - http://www.mtb.uscourts.gov/
- Montana District Court - http://www.mtd.uscourts.gov/

- Nevada Bankruptcy Court - http://www.nvb.uscourts.gov/
- Nevada District Court - http://www.nvd.uscourts.gov/
- Northern Mariana Islands District Court - http://www.nmid.uscourts.gov/
- Office of the Circuit Executive - http://www.ce9.uscourts.gov/
- Oregon Bankruptcy Court - http://www.orb.uscourts.gov/
- Oregon District Court - http://www.ord.uscourts.gov/
- Washington Eastern Bankruptcy Court - http://www.waeb.uscourts.gov/
- Washington Eastern District Court - http://www.waed.uscourts.gov/
- Washington Western Bankruptcy Court - http://www.wawb.uscourts.gov/
- Washington Western District Court - http://www.wawd.uscourts.gov/

10th Circuit

- Bankruptcy Appellate Panel of the Tenth Circuit - http://www.bap10.uscourts.gov/
- Colorado Bankruptcy Court - http://www.cob.uscourts.gov/bindex.htm
- Colorado District Court - http://www.co.uscourts.gov/dindex.htm

- Colorado Federal Courts All Units - http://www.cod.uscourts.gov/
- Court of Appeals - http://www.ca10.uscourts.gov/
- Kansas Bankruptcy Court - http://www.ksb.uscourts.gov/
- Kansas District Court - http://www.ksd.uscourts.gov/
- New Mexico Bankruptcy Court - http://www.nmcourt.fed.us/web/BCDOCS/bcindex.html
- New Mexico District Court - http://www.nmcourt.fed.us/web/DCDOCS/ dcindex.html
- New Mexico Pretrial Services - http://www.nmcourt.fed.us/web/PTDOCS/ptindex.html
- New Mexico Probation Office - http://www.nmcourt.fed.us/web/PBDOCS/pbindex2.html
- Oklahoma Eastern Bankruptcy Court - http://www.okeb.uscourts.gov/
- Oklahoma Eastern District Court - http://www.oked.uscourts.gov/
- Oklahoma Northern Bankruptcy Court - http://www.oknb.uscourts.gov/
- Oklahoma Northern District Court - http://www.oknd.uscourts.gov/
- Oklahoma Western Bankruptcy Court - http://www.okwb.uscourts.gov/
- Oklahoma Western District Court - http://www.okwd.uscourts.gov/
- Utah Bankruptcy Court - http://www.utb.uscourts.gov/
- Utah District Court - http://www.utd.uscourts.gov/
- Wyoming Bankruptcy Court - http://www.wyb.uscourts.gov/
- Wyoming District Court - http://www.wyd.uscourts.gov/

11th Circuit

- Alabama Middle Bankruptcy Court - http://www.almb.uscourts.gov/
- Alabama Middle District Court - http://www.almd.uscourts.gov/
- Alabama Northern Bankruptcy Court - http://www.alnb.uscourts.gov/
- Alabama Northern District Court - http://www.alnd.uscourts.gov/
- Alabama Southern Bankruptcy Court - http://www.alsb.uscourts.gov/
- Alabama Southern District Court - http://www.als.uscourts.gov/
- Court of Appeals - http://www.ca11.uscourts.gov/
- Florida Middle Bankruptcy Court - http://www.flmb.uscourts.gov/
- Florida Middle District Court - http://www.flmd.uscourts.gov/
- Florida Middle Probation Office - http://www.flmp.uscourts.gov/
- Florida Northern Bankruptcy Court - http://www.flnb.uscourts.gov/
- Florida Northern District Court - http://www.flnd.uscourts.gov/

- Florida Northern Probation and Pretrial - http://www.flnp.uscourts.gov/
- Florida Southern Bankruptcy Court - http://www.flsb.uscourts.gov/
- Florida Southern District Court - http://www.flsd.uscourts.gov/
- Georgia Middle Bankruptcy Court - http://www.gamb.uscourts.gov/
- Georgia Middle District Court - http://www.gamd.uscourts.gov/
- Georgia Northern Bankruptcy Court - http://www.ganb.uscourts.gov/
- Georgia Northern District Court - http://www.gand.uscourts.gov/
- Georgia Southern Bankruptcy Court - http://www.gasb.uscourts.gov/
- Georgia Southern District Court - http://www.gasd.uscourts.gov/

DC Circuit

- DC Bankruptcy Court - http://www.dcb.uscourts.gov/
- DC Circuit Court of Appeals - http://www.cadc.uscourts.gov/
- DC District Court - http://www.dcd.uscourts.gov/
- DC Probation Office - http://www.dcp.uscourts.gov/

Federal Circuit

- U.S. Court of Appeals For the Federal Circuit - http://www.cafc.uscourts.gov/

Other

- Federal Judicial Assistants Association - http://fjaa.net/FJAA/FJAA.html
- U.S. Court of International Trade - http://www.cit.uscourts.gov/
- U.S. Supreme Court - http://www.supremecourtus.gov/
- United States Sentencing Commission - http://www.ussc.gov

In: A Journalist's Guide ...
Editor: Lilliana Jones
ISBN: 978-1-63463-382-6

Chapter 2

U.S. CIRCUIT COURT JUDGES: PROFILE OF PROFESSIONAL EXPERIENCES PRIOR TO APPOINTMENT*

Barry J. McMillion

SUMMARY

This report provides an analysis of the professional qualifications and experiences of U.S. circuit court judges who are currently serving on the federal bench. Interest in the professional qualifications of those nominated to the federal judiciary has been demonstrated by Congress and others. Congressional interest in the professional experiences of those nominated by a President to the federal courts reflects, in part, the evaluative role of Congress in examining the qualifications of those who are nominated to life-tenure positions. Other organizations, such as the American Bar Association (ABA), also have an ongoing interest in the professional qualifications of those appointed to the federal judiciary. Additionally, scholars have demonstrated an interest in this topic by examining whether a relationship exists between the professional or career experiences of judges and judicial decision making.

The analysis in this report focuses on the professional experiences of 163 active U.S. circuit court judges who were serving as of February 1,

* This is an edited, reformatted and augmented version of a Congressional Research Service publication R43538, prepared for Members and Committees of Congress dated May 9, 2014.

2014. Active judges are those who have not taken senior status, retired, or resigned. Consequently, the statistics provided do not necessarily reflect all circuit court judges who are *sitting* on the bench (which include judges who have assumed senior status).

Some of this report's findings include the following:

- A majority, 54.6%, of active circuit court judges had prior judicial experience at some point before being appointed as circuit court judges (and 45.4% had no such experience).
  - Of the judges with prior judicial experience, 22.7% served solely as another type of federal judge (e.g., a U.S. district court judge), while 20.9% served solely as a state judge and another 11.0% had both prior federal and state judicial experience.
- A majority, 84.7%, of active circuit court judges had at least some prior experience as an attorney in private practice at some point prior to their appointment as a circuit judge.
  - Of active circuit court judges with private practice experience, a plurality (26.4%) had 15 or more years of experience as an attorney in private practice.
- While 45.4% of active circuit judges do not have prior judicial experience, a much smaller percentage, 15.3%, have no prior experience in private practice.
- Circuit court judges without either prior judicial experience or experience as an attorney in private practice had other professional experiences such as working as an attorney for the federal government or as a law professor.
- Immediately prior to their appointment to the appellate bench, most circuit court judges were either serving as another type of judge or had been engaged in private practice for at least 10 years.
  - Approximately half, 50.3%, of all active circuit judges were serving as another type of judge immediately prior to their appointment (i.e., serving as a district court judge, another type of federal judge such as a bankruptcy judge, or a state judge).
- Approximately one quarter, 25.8%, of active circuit court judges were working as attorneys in private practice immediately prior to being appointed as a circuit judge (with 22.1% having worked in private practice for 10 years or more).

INTRODUCTION

This report provides an analytic overview of the professional experiences and qualifications of those individuals who are currently serving as active U.S.

circuit court judges.[1] Ongoing congressional interest in the professional experiences of judicial nominees reflects, in part, the evaluative role of Congress in examining the qualifications of those who are nominated by the President to life-tenure positions.

Senators, when giving floor speeches supporting circuit court nominations, routinely highlight certain professional experiences or qualifications often considered important to serving as a federal judge. Examples of such statements include the following:

> A Senator noting that a nominee to the Fourth Circuit Court of Appeals had 22 years of prior judicial experience "at the State courts and the Federal courts." The Senator stated that the nominee "has not only served as a distinguished judge, but also he came to the courts as an experienced prosecutor. He was with the Civil Rights Division at the Department of Justice and with the U.S. Attorney's Office in Maryland."[2]
>
> A Senator noting that a nominee to the First Circuit had joined a prestigious law firm in the Senator's home state, "where over the subsequent 32 years [he] specialized in complex civil litigation at both the trial and appellate levels." The Senator also stated that the nominee had served as chairman of the state's Professional Ethics Commission and as president of the state's bar association, and that "his 30-plus years of real-world litigation experience would bring a valuable perspective to the court."[3]
>
> A Senator emphasizing that a nominee to the Seventh Circuit Court of Appeals would "bring almost 12 years of judicial experience" to the bench as a result of her service on the Wisconsin Supreme Court and as a trial judge on the Milwaukee County Circuit Court. The Senator also noted that prior to the nominee's service as a state judge, the nominee had "practiced commercial litigation for 7 years at one of Wisconsin's most prestigious law firms."[4]

The professional experiences of judicial nominees are also of interest to interest groups, particularly professional organizations such as the American Bar Association (ABA).[5] Judicial nominees are evaluated by the ABA's Standing Committee on the Federal Judiciary.[6] The committee's evaluation criteria focus "strictly on professional qualifications: integrity, professional competence and judicial temperament."[7]

The committee "believes that a prospective nominee to the federal bench ordinarily should have at least twelve years' experience in the practice of law" and that "substantial courtroom and trial experience as a lawyer or trial judge is important."[8] The committee also notes, however, that "distinguished accomplishments in the field of law or experience that is similar to in-court trial work ... may compensate for a prospective nominee's lack of substantial courtroom experience."[9] For prospective circuit court nominees, the committee states that "because an appellate judge deals primarily with the review of briefs and the records of lower courts, the committee places somewhat less emphasis on the importance of trial experience as a qualification for the appellate courts."[10]

Additionally, the professional or career experiences of judges prior to the start of their judicial service has also been of interest to scholars examining whether particular professional experiences might influence or explain variation in aspects of judicial decision making (e.g., whether a judge votes in a consistent ideological direction, the sources relied upon by a judge in reaching his or her decisions, whether a judge decides to publish his or her opinions, etc.).[11] For example, one study found that prior judicial experience for U.S. circuit court judges did not influence variation in judicial decision making in terms of the extent a judge voted in a consistent ideological fashion (such prior experience might have been hypothesized to be a source of consistency in judicial voting).[12] Another study found that district court judges whose primary work before becoming a judge involved non-private practice work experience (e.g., working as a government attorney or law professor) were less likely to rely on regulations and other Internal Revenue Service pronouncements in interpreting the federal tax code than judges whose work prior to becoming a judge was predominately as an attorney in private practice.[13]

Other scholars suggest that the lack of career diversity among federal judges might be problematic, in terms of the lack of diversity diminishing the institutional performance of the courts.[14] Specifically, they argue that, given appropriate procedural conditions, "the greater diversity of participation by people of different [professional] backgrounds and experiences, the greater the range of ideas and information contributed to the institutional process."[15] Consequently, in the context of judicial decision making, "judges with varied career experiences bring distinct perspectives to the bench—perspectives that ultimately lead them to make distinct judicial choices—[and] merging jurists with diverse career paths on a particular court ought ... [to] lead to more effective decision making" by that court.[16]

In light of ongoing interest in the professional qualifications of those nominated to circuit court judgeships, this report seeks to inform Congress by providing statistics related to the professional qualifications or experiences of those currently serving on the bench as U.S. circuit court judges.[17]

Specifically, this report provides statistics and analysis related to (1) the percentage of active circuit court judges with judicial experience, as well as the type of judicial experience; (2) the percentage of active circuit court judges with private practice experience, as well as the length of time of such experience; and (3) the percentage of active circuit court judges by professional experience immediately prior to their appointment to a circuit court judgeship.

DATA CAVEATS

Note that the statistics provided in this report are based upon the professional experiences of individuals serving, as of February 1, 2014, as active U.S. circuit court judges. *Consequently, the statistics do not include circuit court judges who, prior to February 1, 2014, had assumed senior status, retired, or resigned.*[18]

The total number of circuit court judges included in the analysis is 163.[19] Consequently, this is the denominator used to calculate most of the statistics included in the report. The analysis is based on information provided by the *Biographical Directory of Federal Judges*.[20]

MOST COMMON TYPES OF PROFESSIONAL EXPERIENCES

Figure 1 provides statistics related to the two most common types of professional experiences of U.S. circuit court judges who are currently serving on the bench—prior judicial experience and experience working as an attorney in private practice.[21] The percentages reported for the two types of experiences are not mutually exclusive, meaning that there is some overlap between the two categories. For example, 47.9% of all active circuit court judges have both prior judicial experience as well as experience as an attorney in private practice (while 9.0% have neither prior judicial nor private practice experience).[22]

Altogether, 54.6% of U.S. circuit court judges who are currently serving had prior experience as another type of judge before their appointment to a circuit court (and 45.4% had no such experience). Of the judges with prior judicial experience, 22.7% served solely as another type of federal judge (e.g., a U.S. district court judge), while 20.9% served solely as a state judge and another 11.0% had both prior federal and state judicial experience. Of the 74 circuit judges with no prior judicial experience, 81.8% had worked as attorneys in private practice, including 39.2% who worked in private practice for 15 or more years (and another 14.9% who worked in private practice for 10 to 14 years).

Although over half of active circuit court judges have prior judicial experience (54.6%), a greater percentage have at least some prior experience as attorneys in private practice (84.7%).[23] Similarly, while 45.6% of active circuit judges do not have prior judicial experience, a much smaller percentage, 15.3%, have no prior experience in private practice.

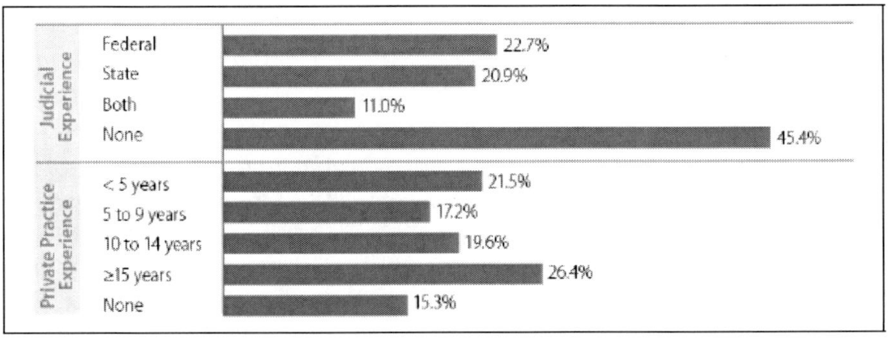

Source: CRS analysis of data provided by the Administrative Office of U.S. Courts.

Note: This figure shows, as of February 1, 2014, the percentage of active U.S. circuit court judges with judicial experience and private practice experience.

Figure 1. Percentage of Active U.S. Circuit Court Judges with Judicial Experience and Private Practice Experience. (as of February 1, 2014).

Figure 1 also shows that of active circuit court judges with private practice experience, a plurality (26.4%) had 15 or more years of experience as attorneys in private practice. Another 21.5% had less than 5 years of experience, while 17.2% had 5 to 9 years of experience and 19.6% had 10 to 14 years of experience. Altogether, 46.0% of active circuit court judges had 10 or more years of experience as attorneys in private practice (while 54.0% had less than 10 years of experience or no private practice experience).[24]

PROFESSIONAL POSITION IMMEDIATELY PRIOR TO APPOINTMENT

Figure 2 reports the percentage of active U.S. circuit court judges who had a particular type of position or occupation immediately prior to their appointment as a circuit court judge.[25] So, for example, a plurality of active circuit court judges, 27.0%, were U.S. district court judges immediately prior to being appointed as circuit court judges. Altogether, half (50.3%) of all active circuit court judges were serving as another type of judge (either a U.S. district court judge, another type of federal judge, or a state judge).[26]

The percentage of circuit court judges serving as another type of judge immediately prior to appointment might be lower than what has been the case, historically, for circuit court judges (at least during the first half of the 20th century). For example, of circuit court judges appointed during the seven presidencies from Theodore Roosevelt to Franklin Roosevelt, 63.7% were serving as another type of judge at the time of appointment or promotion to the U.S. courts of appeals.[27] Additionally, 55.6% and 57.5% of Eisenhower and Johnson circuit court appointees, respectively, were serving as judges prior to their appointment to a circuit court.[28] In general, service as a U.S. district court judge was the most common type of judicial experience of those serving as judges immediately prior to their appointment as a circuit court judge. As noted by one scholar, the "federal district court bench is a training camp for the federal courts of appeals bench. A president faced with a vacancy on a court of appeals looks, though not exclusively, to sitting district court judges."[29]

Of circuit court judges currently serving on the bench, approximately one-quarter (25.8%) were working as attorneys in private practice prior to being appointed as a circuit court judge, with 22.1% having worked in private practice for 10 years or more. Additionally, of those working in private practice for 10 years or more, 80.6% had been working as an attorney in private practice for at least 15 years.

As the percentages reported in *Figure 2* indicate, a relatively large majority of active circuit court judges (72.4%) were, prior to being appointed as circuit judges, serving as either another type of judge or engaged in private practice for 10 or more years (and often for 15 or more years).

Other types of positions held by active U.S. circuit court judges prior to being appointed include working as an attorney at the Department of Justice (DOJ) or a U.S. Attorneys' Office (7.4%) or working as a law professor

(6.7%). Another 9.8% of active circuit court judges held other types of positions immediately prior to being appointed.[30]

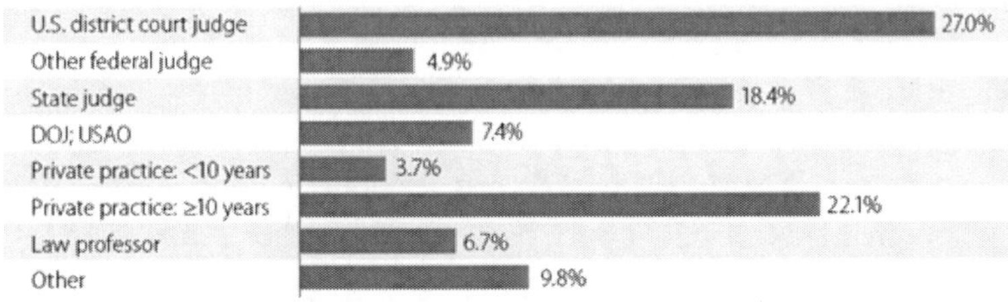

Source: CRS analysis of data provided by the Administrative Office of U.S. Courts.

Note: This figure shows, as of February 1, 2014, the percentage of active U.S. circuit court judges by type of professional position immediately prior to their appointment as a circuit judge.

Figure 2. Percentage of Active U.S. Circuit Court Judges by Type of Professional Position Immediately Prior to Appointment. (as of February 1, 2014).

Of appointees of Democratic Presidents who are currently on the bench, the most common type of position immediately prior to appointment as a circuit court judge was service as another type of judge (54.8% of all active appointees), with a plurality (31.0%) having prior service as a U.S. district court judge. Other types of positions or occupations held by active circuit court appointees of Democratic Presidents immediately prior to appointment were attorneys in private practice (26.2%), attorneys at the Department of Justice or a U.S. Attorney's Office (8.3%), and law professors (6.0%).[31]

Of appointees of Republican Presidents currently on the bench, the most common type of position immediately prior to appointment as a circuit court judge was service as another type of judge (45.6%), with a plurality (22.8%) having served as a U.S. district court judge. Other types of positions or occupations held by active circuit court appointees of Republican Presidents immediately prior to appointment were attorneys in private practice (25.3%), attorneys at the Department of Justice or a U.S. Attorney's Office (6.3%), and law professors (7.6%). Another 15.2% of Republican appointees had another type of position or occupation immediately prior to their appointment.[32]

CONCLUSION

This report provides a statistical overview of the professional qualifications and experiences of active U.S. circuit court judges. Ongoing congressional interest in the professional background of those nominated to the federal bench reflects, in part, the role of Congress in evaluating the qualifications of those who are nominated by the President to life-tenure positions.

As discussed above, a majority of current circuit court judges have prior judicial experience. A greater majority of active circuit judges also have experience working as attorneys in private practice, often for relatively lengthy periods of time. There are, however, judges without either type of experience who have other types of professional experiences such as working as an attorney for the federal government or as a law professor.

End Notes

[1] The analysis in this section provides statistics for active U.S. circuit court judges only (i.e., the professional experiences and qualifications of senior circuit court judges are not included in the analysis). Additionally, as of this writing, such statistics have not been calculated by CRS for active or senior U.S. district court judges.

[2] Sen. Barbara Mikulski, "Executive Session," Remarks in the Senate, Congressional Record, daily edition, November 9, 2009, p.S11274.

[3] Sen. Susan Collins, "Executive Session," Remarks in the Senate, Congressional Record, daily edition, February, 13, 2013, pp.S672-673.

[4] Sen. Orrin Hatch, "Nomination of Diane S. Sykes to be United States Circuit Judge for the Seventh Circuit," Remarks in the Senate, Congressional Record, daily edition, June 24, 2004, p. S7360.

[5] According to the ABA, "in 1953, at the request of President Dwight D. Eisenhower, the ABA committee started to evaluate the professional qualifications of potential nominees to assist him in resisting growing pressure to repay political debts by appointing persons who might not have the professional qualifications to exercise the important responsibilities" of serving as a federal judge. Note that in 2001, "the Bush White House departed from long-standing practices and did not submit names of prospective nominees to [be evaluated by] the Standing Committee in advance of their nomination." Senators serving on the Judiciary Committee, however, "asked the Standing Committee to continue to provide the Judiciary Committee with its evaluations of judicial nominees." American Bar Association, "Frequently Asked Questions About the ABA Standing Committee on the Federal Judiciary," March 2009, available at http://www.americanbar.org/content/dam/aba/migrated/scfedjud/fjcfaq.authcheckdam.pdf. The process of submitting the names of prospective nominees to the Standing Committee for evaluation prior to individuals being nominated has resumed during the Obama presidency.

[6] In evaluating prospective nominees, the committee gives one of three possible ratings: "well qualified," "qualified," and "not qualified." According to past statistics provided by the ABA, as of March 2009, all but 33 of over 2,000 individuals who were formally nominated by Presidents since 1960 were rated as "qualified" or "well qualified." Ibid. For critical perspectives on the ABA's ratings, see Maya Sen, "How Judicial Qualification Ratings May Disadvantage Minority and Female Candidates," Journal of Law and Courts, vol. 2 (2014),

pp. 33, 34 (finding that black and female U.S. district court nominees are more likely to be awarded lower qualification ratings by the ABA, even after matching on education, professional experience, years of legal experience, age, and ideology) (hereafter Sen, "How Judicial Qualification Ratings May Disadvantage"); Susan N. Smelcer et al., "Evaluating the ABA Ratings of Federal Judicial Nominees," Political Research Quarterly, vol. 65 (2012), pp. 827, 836 (finding that, for U.S. circuit court nominees, "all else being equal, a Democratic nominee is more likely to be rated Well Qualified than a similarly qualified Republican nominee"); Susan Brodie Haire, "Rating the Ratings of the American Bar Association Standing Committee on Federal Judiciary," Justice System Journal, vol. 22 (2001), pp. 1, 15 (finding that, for U.S. circuit court nominees, "caucasian males were more likely to receive a higher rating when compared to minorities or females, even after controlling for length of legal and judicial experiences. Overall, this analysis suggests an inherent bias in the rating process that favors traditional, establishment candidates" to the federal courts).

[7] American Bar Association, Standing Committee on the Federal Judiciary, "What It Is and How It Works," 2009, p. 1, available at http://www.americanbar.org/content/dam/aba/ migrated/ 2011_build/federal_judiciary/ federal_judiciary09.authcheckdam.pdf.

[8] Ibid., p. 3.

[9] Ibid.

[10] Ibid. Note that the committee also states that it "believes that prospective appellate court nominees should possess an especially high degree of legal scholarship, academic talent, analytical and writing abilities, and overall excellence. The ability to write clearly and persuasively, to harmonize a body of law, and to give meaningful guidance to the trial courts and the bar for future cases are particularly important skills for prospective nominees to" circuit court judgeships.

[11] See, for example, Deborah Jones Merritt & James J. Brudney, "Stalking Secret Law: What Predicts Publication in the United States Courts of Appeals," Vanderbilt Law Review, vol. 54 (2001), pp. 71, 84-85 (finding that judges with prior experience representing management were significantly less likely to publish their opinions, perhaps because such judges "have more experience implementing the NLRA [National Labor Relations Act] than judges lacking a management background"); Gregory C. Sisk et al., "Charting the Influences on the Judicial Mind: An Empirical Study of Judicial Reasoning," New York University Law Review, vol. 73 (1998), pp. 1377, 1420-21 (finding that judges with criminal defense experience are more likely to invalidate federal sentencing guidelines than those without such experience); Orley Ashenfelter et al., "Politics and the Judiciary: The Influence of Judicial Background on Case Outcomes," Journal of Legal Studies, vol. 24 (1995), p. 257 (finding no relationship between whether U.S. district court judges had prior judicial experience and judicial outcomes, e.g., whether judges rule for or against a plaintiff); Sheldon Goldman, "Voting Behavior on the United States Courts of Appeals Revisited," American Political Science Review, vol. 69 (1975), pp. 491, 499-500 (generally finding no relationship between whether a U.S. circuit court judge had judicial experience on another court prior to appointment on the appeals court or public prosecutorial experience and his or her voting behavior on various categories of cases; but finding a statistically significant result suggesting that judges without previous judicial experience tended to dissent at a higher rate than those with such experience); S. Sidney Ulmer, "Social Background as an Indicator to the Votes of Supreme Court Justices in Criminal Cases: 1947- 1956 Terms," American Journal of Political Science, vol. 17 (1973), pp. 622, 623-24 (finding that justices with federal administrative experience voted more conservatively than

justices without such experience); Kenneth N. Vines, "Federal District Judges and Race Relations Cases in the South," Journal of Politics, vol. 26 (1964), p. 338 (finding evidence that judges who held state political office were more negatively disposed toward race relations cases than judges who did not hold such positions).

[12] Erin B. Kaheny et al., "Change over Tenure: Voting, Variance, and Decision Making on the U.S. Courts of Appeals," American Journal of Political Science, vol. 52 (2008), pp. 490, 493, 497.

[13] Daniel M. Schneider, "Empirical Research on Judicial Reasoning: Statutory Interpretation in Federal Tax Cases," New Mexico Law Review, vol. 31 (2001), pp. 325, 347.

[14] Lee Epstein et al., "The Norm of Prior Judicial Experience and Its Consequences for Career Diversity on the U.S. Supreme Court," California Law Review, vol. 91 (2003), p. 903.

[15] Ibid., p. 944.

[16] Ibid., p. 956.

[17] As of this writing, CRS has not compiled and analyzed similar data for active district court judges who are currently serving on the bench.

[18] Senior status judges are those judges who have retired from full-time service but continue, on a part-time basis, to hear cases or perform other duties related to judicial administration. Senior status eligibility is based upon a judge's age as well as his or her length of service as an Article III judge. Specifically, beginning at age 65, a judge may retire from office or take senior status after performing 15 years of active service as an Article III judge. A sliding scale of increasing age and decreasing service results in eligibility for retirement compensation at age 70 with a minimum 10 years of service.

[19] As of February 1, 2014, there were 16 vacant U.S. circuit court judgeships. These vacancies are not included in the statistics provided in the report.

[20] Consequently, the data analyzed are limited to information provided by the Directory. The Directory is maintained by the Administrative Office of U.S. Courts and is available at http://www.uscourts.gov/JudgesAndJudgeships/ BiographicalDirectoryOfJudges.aspx.

[21] Some organizations have called for broadening the professional diversity of judges serving on the federal bench. The Alliance for Justice, for example, has recently called upon the President to nominate individuals with experience working as attorneys for public interest organizations. Alliance for Justice, "Broadening the Bench: Professional Diversity and Judicial Nominations," February 6, 2014, available at http://www.afj.org/wp-content/uploads/2014/02/prof-diversity-report-3.2.2014-FINAL-Updated-with-Noms-Through-2.6.14.pdf.

[22] The lack of a nominee's experience in a traditional legal occupation (such as an attorney in private practice) has, in some cases, led some Senators to oppose the nominee's nomination. For example, J. Harvie Wilkinson III was nominated by President Reagan to the Fourth Circuit on January 30, 1984. At the time, Senator Edward M. Kennedy stated, during the debate to invoke cloture on the nomination, that the nominee was "the least qualified nominee ever submitted for an appellate court vacancy." Senators' opposition to the nomination were based, in part, on the nominee's relatively young age (he was 39) and the fact that he had never practiced law. When nominated, Judge Wilkinson was a law professor at the University of Virginia and he had previously worked for a year as a Deputy Assistant Attorney General during the Reagan presidency. Linda Greenhouse, "Reagan Names 6 To Federal Appeals Courts," New York Times, August 2, 1984, available at http://www. nytimes.com/1984/08/02/us/reagan-names-6-to-federal-appealscourts.html.

[23] At least one study has found that judicial nominees receiving the highest ABA ratings include those with previous judicial experience and/or nominees with more years of legal practice experience. Sen, "How Judicial Qualification Ratings May Disadvantage," p. 42.

[24] Overall, 89 of 163 circuit court judges included in the analysis had prior judicial experience (37 of the 89 had only federal experience, 34 only state experience, and 18 had served as a judge for both federal and state courts). Of the 163 judges, 74 had no prior judicial experience. For private practice experience, 138 of 163 judges had some experience as an attorney in private practice (while 25 had none). Of those with private practice experience, 43 had 15 or more years of experience, 32 had 10 to 14 years of experience, 28 had 5 to 9 years of experience, and 35 had less than 5 years of experience.

[25] Of the 163 active U.S. circuit court judges included in the analysis, 44 had been a U.S. district court judge immediately prior to their appointment, 8 had been another type of federal judge, 30 had been a state judge, 12 had been working as an attorney at the Department of Justice or in a U.S. Attorney's Office, 6 had been working in private practice for less than 10 years, 36 had been working in private practice for more than 10 years, 11 had been working as a law professor, and 16 had other types of positions.

[26] Other types of federal judges included in the analysis were U.S. bankruptcy judges and U.S. magistrate judges.

[27] Rayman L. Solomon, "The Politics of Appointment and the Federal Courts' Role in Regulating America: U.S. Courts of Appeals Judgeships from T.R. to F.D.R.," American Bar Foundation Research Journal, vol. 9 (1984), pp. 285, 304. As indicated by the article, the percentage of circuit court appointees who were another type of judge at the time of being appointed or promoted to a circuit court judgeship, by President in chronological order, were 78.6% (T. Roosevelt), 75.0% (Taft), 52.6% (Wilson), 83.3% (Harding), 75.0% (Coolidge), 85.7% (Hoover), and 47.7% (F.D.R.).

[28] In contrast, 47.6% of President Kennedy's circuit court appointees were judges immediately prior to their appointment or promotion to U.S. circuit courts of appeals. Sheldon Goldman, "Characteristics of Eisenhower and Kennedy Appointees to the Lower Federal Courts," Western Political Quarterly, vol. 18 (1965), pp. 755, 758. See also Sheldon Goldman, "Johnson and Nixon Appointees to Lower Federal Courts: Some Socio-Political Perspectives," Journal of Politics, vol. 34 (1972), pp. 934, 936.

[29] Karen Swenson, "Promotion of District Court Judges to the U.S. Courts of Appeals: Explaining President Reagan's Promotions of His Own Appointees," Justice System Journal, vol. 27 (2006), p. 208. Swenson examined whether Presidents seek to reward district court judges who vote the "right" way. She concludes that, "at least for Reagan-appointed judges considered ... , the most convincing conclusion to draw from these data is that district judges' records of conservative voting and support for the federal government, relative to their benchmates, are irrelevant to the president's decision" to nominate the district court judge to a vacant circuit court judgeship. Instead, the "decision to elevate a district judge may be ... influenced by factors not measured [in the article], such as pressure from a key senator or two, close friends of the president, or high-ranking officials in the president's party." Ibid., p. 217.

[30] Examples of other types of positions that circuit court judges held immediately prior to their appointment include state attorney general; deputy general counsel of a research university; assistant to the President of the United States and staff secretary; deputy secretary and general counsel of a state agency; and deputy secretary of a U.S. federal executive department.24 Overall, 89 of 163 circuit court judges included in the analysis had prior judicial experience (37 of the 89 had only federal experience, 34 only state experience, and

18 had served as a judge for both federal and state courts). Of the 163 judges, 74 had no prior judicial experience. For private practice experience, 138 of 163 judges had some experience as an attorney in private practice (while 25 had none). Of those with private practice experience, 43 had 15 or more years of experience, 32 had 10 to 14 years of experience, 28 had 5 to 9 years of experience, and 35 had less than 5 years of experience.

[31] The specific number of judges by the type of experience immediately prior to appointment and by party of the appointing President are available from the author upon request.

[32] Examples of Republican appointees included in the "other" category are Judge Danny L. Boggs (Reagan appointee, position immediately prior to appointment was Deputy Secretary of Energy); Judge Edward E. Carnes (G.H.W. Bush appointee, Asst. Attorney General, Alabama); and Judge Lavenski R. Smith (G.W. Bush appointee, Arkansas Public Service Commissioner).

In: A Journalist's Guide …
Editor: Lilliana Jones

ISBN: 978-1-63463-382-6

Chapter 3

LENGTH OF TIME FROM NOMINATION TO CONFIRMATION FOR U.S. CIRCUIT AND DISTRICT COURT NOMINEES: OVERVIEW AND POLICY OPTIONS TO SHORTEN THE PROCESS*

Barry J. McMillion

SUMMARY

The process by which lower federal court judges are nominated by the President and considered by the Senate is of continuing interest to Congress. Recent Senate debate over judicial nominations has frequently concerned whether a particular President's judicial nominees, relative to the nominees of other recent Presidents, waited longer for their nominations to be considered by the Senate. This report addresses this issue by (1) providing a statistical analysis of the time from nomination to confirmation for U.S. circuit and district court nominees from Presidents Reagan to Obama; (2) identifying possible consequences of a protracted confirmation process for circuit and district court nominees; and (3) identifying policy options the Senate might consider to shorten the length

* This is an edited, reformatted and augmented version of a Congressional Research Service publication R43316, prepared for Members and Committees of Congress, dated November 20, 2013.

of time from nomination to confirmation for lower federal court nominees.

In general, the mean (average) and median number of days from nomination to confirmation increased during each presidency since President Reagan. For circuit court nominees confirmed during a President's time in office (whether one or two terms), the average number of days elapsed from nomination to confirmation ranged from 68.7 days during the Reagan presidency to 350.6 days during George W. Bush's presidency. The median number of days from nomination to confirmation for circuit court nominees confirmed ranged from 45 days (Reagan) to 229 days (Obama).

For district court nominees, the average time between nomination and confirmation ranged from 67.9 days (Reagan) to 220.8 days (Obama). For district court nominees, the median time elapsed ranged from a low of 41 days (Reagan) to 215 days (Obama).

There are several potential consequences of a protracted confirmation process for lower federal court nominees. These include (1) consistently high vacancy rates for circuit and district court judgeships as well as a greater number of such vacancies considered "judicial emergencies" by the Judicial Conference of the United States; (2) detrimental effects on the management of the federal courts, including judicial caseloads; (3) greater difficulty in finding highly qualified individuals who are willing to be nominated to the federal bench; (4) the politicization of the confirmation process in a manner that might leave the public with the impression that the ideological or partisan predisposition of the nominee is the primary consideration in determining how the nominee will approach his or her work on the bench.

Three policy options discussed in the report include the following:

- Utilizing time frames for various stages of the confirmation process for U.S. circuit and district court nominees, including the length of time from nomination to committee hearing as well as the length of time from committee report to final Senate action.
- Expediting the confirmation process for judicial nominations using "fast-track" procedures. Such procedures might include classifying some judicial nominations as "privileged nominations" as is currently done to expedite Senate consideration of nominations to some positions in the executive branch.
- Treating district court nominations differently than circuit court nominations by changing certain features of the confirmation process for district court nominations. Such changes might result in shortening the time from nomination to confirmation for district court nominees.

INTRODUCTION

In recent years a subject of continuing interest to Senators has been the length of time taken for lower federal court nominations to receive Senate confirmation.[1] Senate debate often has concerned whether a President's judicial nominees, relative to the nominees of other recent Presidents, encountered more difficulty or had to wait longer before receiving consideration by the Senate Judiciary Committee or up-or-down floor votes on confirmation.[2] Of related concern to the Senate have been recent increases in the number and percentage of vacant judgeships in the federal judiciary and the effect of delays in the processing of judicial nominations on filling such vacancies.[3]

This report seeks to inform the current debate in three ways: first, by providing an overview of the time taken by the Senate during recent presidencies to confirm U.S. circuit and district court nominees; second, by identifying potential consequences of a protracted confirmation process for such nominees; and third, by identifying policy options the Senate might consider to shorten the length of time from nomination to confirmation for U.S. circuit and district court nominees. It is comprised of four sections:

- A first section provides background information related to U.S. circuit and district courts, the two types of lower federal courts to which a President frequently makes nominations.
- A second section provides the average and median lengths of time from nomination to confirmation for circuit and district court nominees of the five most recent Presidents (i.e., Presidents Reagan to Obama).[4] The average and median waiting times from nomination to confirmation, the section concludes, generally increased from one presidency to the next for both circuit and district court nominees.[5] This section also discusses the adoption of a new standing order in the 113th Congress that might serve to facilitate negotiations arranging for floor consideration of district court nominees (and, thus, might also shorten the length of time district court nominees wait to have their nominations considered by the full Senate).
- A third section identifies possible consequences of the relatively longer periods of time lower federal court nominees have waited, once nominated, to be confirmed by the Senate.

- A fourth section identifies and analyzes three policy options the Senate might consider in order to shorten the time from nomination to confirmation for at least some circuit and district court nominees.

This report does not take the position that all judicial nominations should be processed relatively quickly by the Senate. There might be instances in which heightened scrutiny of U.S. circuit and district court nominees by the Senate is warranted, leading to relatively long waiting times from nomination to confirmation for these nominees.[6] Additionally, given that there are no minimal qualifications or term limits for Article III judges, some Senators might argue that the emphasis of the confirmation process should be to avoid "rubber stamping" judicial nominations submitted by the President,[7] even if, presumably, such deliberate processing by the Senate leads to longer wait times for nominees to be confirmed.

Article III Lower Courts

Article III, Section I of the Constitution provides, in part, that the "judicial Power of the United States, shall be vested in one supreme Court, and in such inferior Courts as the Congress may from time to time ordain and establish." It further provides that Justices on the Supreme Court and judges on lower courts established by Congress under Article III have what effectively has come to mean life tenure, holding office "during good Behaviour."[8] Along with the Supreme Court, some other courts that constitute Article III courts in the federal system are the U.S. courts of appeals, the U.S. district courts, and the U.S. Court of International Trade.

As mentioned above, this report concerns nominations to the U.S. circuit courts of appeals and the U.S. district courts (including the territorial district courts). Outside the report's scope are nominations to the U.S. Supreme Court and the occasional nominations that Presidents make to the nine-member U.S. Court of International Trade.

U.S. Courts of Appeals

The U.S. courts of appeals take appeals from federal district court decisions and also review the decisions of many administrative agencies. Cases presented to the courts of appeals are generally considered by judges sitting in three-member panels. Courts within the courts of appeals system are often called "circuit courts" (e.g., the First Circuit Court of Appeals is also referred to simply as the "First Circuit"), because the nation is divided into 12 geographic circuits, each with a U.S. court of appeals. One additional nationwide circuit, the Federal Circuit, hears certain specialized legal claims. Altogether, 179 appellate court judgeships for these 13 courts of appeals are currently authorized by law. The First Circuit (comprising Maine, Massachusetts, New Hampshire, Rhode Island, and Puerto Rico) has the fewest number of authorized appellate court judgeships, 6, while the Ninth Circuit (comprising Alaska, Arizona, California, Hawaii, Idaho, Montana, Nevada, Oregon, and Washington) has the most, 29.

In this report, nominations to U.S. courts of appeals judgeships are frequently referred to as "circuit court nominations."

U.S. District Courts

U.S. district courts are the federal trial courts of general jurisdiction. There are 91 Article III district courts: 89 in the 50 states, plus one in the District of Columbia and one more in Puerto Rico. Each state has at least one U.S. district court, while some states (specifically California, New York, and Texas) have as many as four. Altogether, 673 Article III U.S. district court judgeships are currently authorized by law. Congress has authorized between 1 and 28 judgeships for each district court. The Eastern District of Oklahoma has 1 judgeship (the smallest number among Article III district courts), while the Southern District of New York and the Central District of California each have 28 judgeships (the most among Article III district courts).

Additionally, there are three U.S. territorial courts established by Congress pursuant to its authority to govern the territories under Article IV of the Constitution. Judicial appointees to these courts serve 10-year terms, with one judgeship each in Guam and the Northern Mariana Islands, and two in the U.S. Virgin Islands.[9]

In sum, references throughout this report to U.S. district court judgeships include a total of 677 judgeships (673 Article III judgeships, of which 10 are temporary, and 4 territorial judgeships).

LENGTH OF TIME FROM NOMINATION TO CONFIRMATION FOR JUDICIAL NOMINEES ACROSS RECENT PRESIDENCIES

This section provides statistics related to the length of time it has taken for circuit and district court nominees, once nominated by the President, to be confirmed by the Senate.[10] Figure 1 tracks by President, from Reagan to Obama, the mean (average) and median number of days from nomination to confirmation for all circuit and district court nominees confirmed during a President's tenure in office (whether one or two terms).[11] In general, the average and median time from nomination to confirmation has increased during each presidency since President Reagan.

If a nominee was nominated more than once by a President, prior to the nominee's eventual confirmation by the Senate, the first date on which he or she was nominated was used to calculate the days elapsed from nomination to confirmation. Note that the average and median number of days from nomination to confirmation can reflect various factors, including opposition by the minority party in the Senate,[12] committee and floor scheduling decisions unrelated to partisan opposition to the nomination, and delays in receiving requested background information from nominees.[13]

U.S. Circuit Court Nominees

As shown in *Figure 1*, President George W. Bush's circuit court nominees who were confirmed during his two terms waited, on average, the longest period of time from first nomination to confirmation (350.6 days). As of November 1, 2013, President Obama's nominees waited, on average, the second-longest period of time (257 days) followed by the circuit court nominees of Presidents Clinton (238.2 days), George H.W. Bush (103.7 days), and Reagan (68.7 days).[14]

President G.W. Bush's circuit nominees waited, *on average*, the longest period of time from nomination to confirmation while President Obama's circuit court nominees have, thus far, had the longest *median* wait time from first nomination to confirmation (229 days).[15] This statistic is interpreted to mean that half of the circuit court nominees who have been confirmed during President Obama's time in office (as of November 1, 2013) waited more than 229 days from nomination to confirmation, while the other half waited less than 229 days.

The circuit court nominees who were confirmed during President G.W. Bush's tenure had the second longest median wait time (216 days)[16] followed, in decreasing order, by the circuit court nominees of President Clinton (139 days), G.H.W. Bush (85.5 days), and Reagan (45 days).

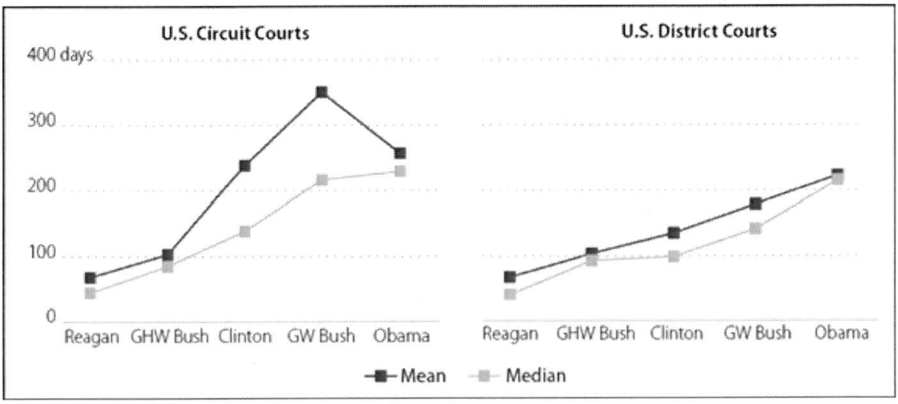

Source: Internal CRS judicial nominations database.

Note: This figure shows, for each of the past five Presidents, the mean and median number of days from first nomination to confirmation for all U.S. circuit and district court nominees who were confirmed during a President's tenure (whether one or two terms). The statistics for nominees during the Obama presidency are current through November 1, 2013.

Figure 1.U.S. Circuit and District Court Nominees of Five Most Recent Presidents: Mean and Median Number of Days from Nomination to Confirmation.

U.S. District Court Nominees

Turning again to **Figure 1**, President Obama's confirmed nominees for district courts waited, on average, 220.8 days from nomination to confirmation. President G.W. Bush's district nominees waited, on average, 178.8 days. The district court nominees confirmed during President Clinton's two terms waited an average of 135 days while the nominees of Presidents G.H.W. Bush and Reagan waited on average 103.8 and 67.9 days, respectively.[17]

The median waiting times from nomination to confirmation for district court nominees ranged from a high of 215 days, thus far, during President Obama's time in office to a low of 41 days during President Reagan's two terms. The median waiting times from nomination to confirmation for district court nominees of the remaining three Presidents were 141.5 days (G.W. Bush), 99 days (Clinton), and 93 days (G.H.W. Bush).[18]

Perhaps in response to the relatively longer waiting times experienced by President Obama's district court nominees, the Senate adopted a new standing order in the 113th Congress that might serve to facilitate negotiations arranging for floor consideration of district court nominations (and, thus, might serve to shorten the length of time district court nominees wait to have their nominations considered by the full Senate once their nominations are reported by the Judiciary Committee).[19]

The standing order provides for a new procedure in effect for just the 113th Congress by which the Senate could move more quickly to final action on district court nominations supported by at least three-fifths of the Senate. Specifically, if cloture is invoked on a district court nomination in accordance with Rule XXII of the Senate, post-cloture consideration is reduced from a maximum of 30 hours to 2 hours.[20] Generally, district court nominations are considered pursuant to unanimous consent agreements. The majority leader, when the new standing order was approved, indicated that the intent is to continue to negotiate unanimous consent agreements for the consideration of such nominations[21]—which might be facilitated by the alternative provided by the standing order.[22]

As of November 2013, an insufficient number of district court nominations have been considered since the beginning of the 113th Congress to measure whether the standing order has been effective in shortening the length of time to confirm such nominations. If it is determined in the future that the standing order is useful in shortening the time from nomination to confirmation for district court nominees, the Senate might consider renewing it on a temporary basis for future congresses (or making it permanent).

POSSIBLE CONSEQUENCES OF LONGER WAITING TIMES FROM NOMINATION TO CONFIRMATION

In recent years, scholars and others concerned with the judicial appointment process have identified possible consequences of relatively long waiting times from nomination to confirmation experienced by judicial nominees.[23] Five of the more notable possible consequences are discussed below.

Increase in Vacancy Rates of Circuit and District Court Judgeships

A protracted confirmation process might contribute to an increase in vacancy rates for U.S. circuit and district court judgeships as well as an increase in the number of vacancies considered "judicial emergencies" by the Judicial Conference of the United States.[24] In recent years there have been several episodes of "historically high" vacancy rates for U.S. circuit and district court judgeships.[25] Such periods in which vacancy rates have increased to historically high levels have occurred during presidencies in which, as shown in *Figure 1,* the length of time it takes to confirm circuit and district court nominees has similarly increased.

Additionally, as reported previously by CRS, President Obama is the only White House occupant since at least President Reagan for whom the district court vacancy rate increased during a presidential first term unaccompanied by the creation of new district court judgeships.[26] Such an increase in the vacancy rate coincided, during President Obama's first term, with historically high average and median waiting times from nomination to confirmation for U.S. district court nominees.[27]

Detrimental Effects on Judicial Administration

If longer waiting times from nomination to confirmation are associated with higher vacancy rates, then longer waiting times might also have a detrimental effect on the management of the federal courts, and on caseload management in particular. Such an effect might disproportionately impact those courts with relatively heavier caseloads.[28]

Such a relationship between longer waiting times and a decline in the quality or efficiency of judicial administration has been suggested by Chief Justice John G. Roberts, Jr., as well as by his predecessor, Chief Justice William Rehnquist. Chief Justice Roberts, noting that vacancies are not evenly distributed across judicial districts, has stated that "a persistent problem has developed in the process of filling judicial vacancies.... This has created acute difficulties for some judicial districts. Sitting judges in those districts have been burdened with extraordinary caseloads."[29] Consequently, he has argued that there is "an urgent need for the political branches to find a longterm solution to this recurring problem."[30]

Similarly, former Chief Justice Rehnquist argued that "[j]udicial vacancies can contribute to a backlog of cases, undue delays in civil cases, and stopgap measures to shift judicial personnel where they are most needed. Vacancies cannot remain at such high levels indefinitely without eroding the quality of justice that traditionally has been associated with the federal judiciary."[31] He emphasized the need to more quickly fill judicial vacancies, arguing "[T]o continue functioning effectively and efficiently, our federal courts must be appropriately staffed. This means that judicial vacancies must be filled in a timely manner with well-qualified candidates.... We [the judiciary] simply ask that the President nominate qualified candidates with reasonable promptness and that the Senate act within a reasonable time to confirm or reject them."[32]

Fewer Highly Qualified Nominees

Fewer qualified individuals might be willing to be nominated because of the protracted length of time it takes to be confirmed. A relatively lengthy time from nomination to confirmation might interfere with professional and personal obligations of potential nominees. Such interference might cause some qualified individuals to forgo the opportunity to serve on the federal bench.

Such interference might be particularly problematic for nominees working in private practice. As Justice Rehnquist noted, "[A] drawn-out and uncertain confirmation process is a handicap to judicial recruitment across the board, but it most significantly restricts the universe of lawyers in private practice who are willing to be nominated for a federal judgeship.... for lawyers coming directly from private practice, there is both a strong financial disincentive and the possibility of losing clients in the course of the wait for a confirmation vote."[33]

Another observer argues that, in terms of the protracted periods of time that some recent nominees have waited for a Senate vote after being reported by the Judiciary Committee, "[T]he cost to nominees is real. They and their families find it stressful. For nominees in private practice, the delay is expensive as their work dries up. For nominees who are serving as state or magistrate judges, there is also a cost to the efficiency of the courts on which the nominees are sitting at the time of nomination, as the delay creates uncertainty and difficulty for their litigants."[34] Such difficulties might lead some individuals, who would otherwise be highly qualified nominees for the federal bench, to pass on the opportunity to be nominated.[35]

Excessive Emphasis on the Ideological or Partisan Predisposition of Nominees

Longer waiting times from nomination to confirmation might politicize the confirmation process in a way that leaves the public with the impression that the ideological or partisan predisposition of the nominee is the primary consideration in determining how the nominee will approach his or her work on the bench. A former chief judge of the Fifth Circuit Court of Appeals, for example, has argued as much, stating that "a highly partisan or ideological judicial selection process conveys the notion to the electorate that judges are simply another breed of political agents, that judicial decisions should be in accord with political ideology, all of which tends to undermine public confidence in the legitimacy of the courts."[36]

For district court nominees in particular, the impression by the public that trial judges routinely act based on their partisan or ideological predisposition might be at odds with the reality of the type of work they typically do while on the bench. For example, former Attorney General Nicholas Katzenbach has argued that "[m]ost trial lawyers will say that the political or ideological views of a trial judge are not very important. What is important is his experience with litigation, his demeanor on the bench, and the fairness of his rulings on evidence."[37]

Other Potential Consequences

Finally, a confirmation process characterized by longer waiting times might adversely affect the Senate in ways not directly related to the confirmation process itself. For example, a protracted confirmation process characterized by partisan or ideological rancor might have a "spill-over" effect of politicizing issues related to the judiciary that might otherwise enjoy bipartisan support, such as "legislation that could affect the independent operation of the federal courts (court funding, judicial salaries, jurisdiction),"[38] as well as leading to "substantive [congressional] intrusions on adjudicatory functions ... "[39]

Policy Options for Shortening the Time from Nomination to Confirmation

This section discusses three proposals to shorten the amount of time, generally, from nomination to confirmation for U.S. circuit and district court nominees.[40] These proposals are not mutually exclusive and any policy adopted by the Senate to shorten the length of time from nomination to confirmation for judicial nominees might incorporate elements of more than one of the proposals.

As the scope of this report includes only the time from nomination to confirmation, this section does not include proposals that have been offered to reform or change the pre-nomination stage of the judicial confirmation process.[41] This section, furthermore, does not provide an exhaustive list or description of potential policies that might be adopted by the Senate to shorten the time from nomination to confirmation for lower federal court nominees.[42]

Imposition of Time Tables on the Confirmation Process

The Senate might consider adopting a time table for one or more stages of the nomination process. Such time tables would establish deadlines for Senate action on judicial nominations.

Both Presidents G.W. Bush and Obama, for example, have offered such proposals. Specifically, in 2002, President G.W. Bush proposed two deadlines: a nominee would (1) receive a hearing before the Senate Judiciary Committee within 90 days of being nominated, and (2) receive an up-ordown vote in the Senate within 180 days of being nominated.[43] President Bush, in proposing the deadlines, argued that a "strict deadline is the best way to ensure that judicial nominees are promptly and fairly considered. And 90 days is more than enough time for the committee to conduct necessary research before holding a hearing." Additionally, he maintained that the 180 days deadline for final Senate action "is a very generous period of time that will allow all the Senators to evaluate nominees and have their votes counted."[44] For his part, President Obama has not offered a deadline for nominees to receive a hearing but instead called for a Senate rule that would require all judicial (and executive) nominees to receive an up-or-down vote by the full Senate within 90 days of being nominated.[45]

Such proposals have not come solely from Presidents.[46] In 2004, Senator Arlen Specter of Pennsylvania introduced a resolution providing for a series of time tables or deadlines for Senate action on judicial nominations.[47] The three deadlines proposed by Senate Specter required (1) the Judiciary Committee to hold a hearing on the nomination within 30 days after the nomination was submitted to the Senate; (2) the committee to act on the nomination within 30 days of the hearing; and (3) the full Senate act on the nomination within 30 days after the committee reported out the nomination. The proposal also authorized the committee chair and the Senate majority leader to extend the period for committee and full Senate action, respectively, by up to an additional 30 days for cause. Presumably, however, the maximum amount of time from nomination to final Senate action for most nominees would not exceed 90 days.[48]

One concern that the Senate might have in adopting time tables is the question of enforcement (i.e., how would the Senate ensure that such time tables are followed and would there be any consequences if deadlines are not met?) Second, the Senate might be concerned that, by committing itself to certain deadlines, it would give a President greater leverage or influence in the selection of judicial nominees. During the G.W. Bush presidency, for example, CRS noted that streamlining the confirmation process with various timelines "could tip the balance of power on the selection of [judicial] nominees toward the President."[49] Another concern might be that time tables would, instead, result in lengthening the time from nomination to confirmation for some nominations. For example, Jane Kelly, a recent nominee to the Eighth Circuit Court of Appeals, was confirmed by the Senate on April 24, 2013—83 days after being nominated by President Obama on January 31, 2013. The imposition of a rigid time table on nominations such as the Kelly nomination (which are uncontroversial) might have the unintended result of lengthening the amount of time from nomination to confirmation for such nominees.

Fast-Track Certain Nominations

In addition to imposing deadlines on various stages of the confirmation process, the Senate might also consider mechanisms that would enable some judicial nominations to be more quickly acted upon by the full Senate (i.e., receive "fast-track" treatment after the nomination is submitted by the President). Such fast-track treatment might involve the Senate (by statute, standing order or rule) committing to process certain nominations within a certain amount of time after they are submitted by the President.

One proposal involves giving fast-track consideration to nominees recommended by bipartisan commissions in their home states.[50] If the President selects an individual from a list of candidates recommended by a bipartisan commission, then the nominee would be given fast-track "protection" during the confirmation process. If, however, the President selects someone not recommended by a bipartisan commission, the nomination would not be given fast-track consideration by the Senate. While such bipartisan commissions are currently used by some Senators,[51] the empirical evidence from President Obama's first term does not suggest that nominees selected by commissions are confirmed more quickly than nominees from states without such commissions.[52]

Another option available to the Senate is to consider some judicial nominations as "privileged nominations" for the purpose of potentially shortening the time from nomination to confirmation. Such an approach was recently adopted by the Senate during the 112th Congress for nominations to 272 positions across various Cabinet agencies, oversight boards and advisory councils, and independent agencies. Specifically, S.Res. 116, approved by the Senate on June 29, 2011, provides for an alternative confirmation process of nominations to these particular positions. This new approach allows these nominations to bypass formal committee consideration unless a single Senator objects to using the expedited process. The positions included in the resolution tend not to be those associated with controversy and their nominations in the past typically have required little individual floor debate for confirmation.[53]

The specific provisions of S.Res. 116 provide that once the Senate receives a nomination to one of the specified 272 positions, it is placed on the Senate's *Executive Calendar* as a "privileged nomination." Although the nomination is not formally referred to committee, the committee is still responsible for gathering biographical and financial information used to evaluate the nominee. After the chair of the committee of jurisdiction notifies, in writing, the Senate's executive clerk that all the information requested has been received, the nomination remains on the list of "privileged nominations" for 10 session days before being moved to the list of "nominations" on the *Executive Calendar*.

At any time from when the Senate receives the nomination to when the nomination is placed on the list of "nominations" on the calendar (i.e., while the nomination is still pending on the "privileged nominations" list), any Senator can request that the nomination be referred to committee, and not be considered using the new process. The nomination then proceeds using the existing confirmation process, beginning with referral to committee. In this manner, S.Res. 116 utilizes the existing practices of the Senate's unanimous consent process, where objection from even one Senator will prevent the new process from being used.

Adopting such a resolution for some judicial nominations might have the effect of shortening the time from nomination to confirmation. While the Senate Judiciary Committee would retain its information-gathering function (and Senators on the committee would be able to signal to other Senators their approval or disapproval of the nominations through informal discussions and floor speeches), removing the committee's need to act on these nominations might expedite the process for nominations that are uncontroversial and would receive unanimous support by the full Senate.[54]

The most likely Article III judicial nominations that would be suitable for such an approach are nominations to U.S. district court judgeships.[55] The Senate might afford privileged status using any number of criteria, including whether the nomination was recommended by a bipartisan commission in the nominee's home state; whether the nomination has the support of at least one home state Senator of the opposite party as the President; or whether the nomination is for a vacancy qualifying as a "judicial emergency" by the Judicial Conference of the United States. The Senate might also decide to allow a fixed percentage of U.S. district court nominations to go through the confirmation process as privileged nominations. The Senate, for example, might allow 25% of all district court nominations during any given year to be submitted as privileged nominations;[56] such an approach might, across different presidencies, provide for uniformity, predictability, and relatively speedy Senate approval of certain nominations that are uncontroversial and are supported by all Senators.[57]

Treating some judicial nominations as privileged nominations, however, might raise concerns for at least some Senators. First, some Members might be concerned about preserving the role of the Judiciary Committee in having its say on every judicial nomination submitted by the President, including those considered routine or uncontroversial. Second, Senators might not want to signal potential problems with a judicial nomination by requesting that it be taken off the list of privileged nominations on the *Calendar* and instead be sent to committee. Third, a Senator desiring to lengthen the regular confirmation process for a nominee could do so by waiting to object to the new process until the nomination had been listed for nine days of session on the *Calendar* as a privileged nomination (and for which all information had been received). The objection would re-start the confirmation process to its initial stages, referral to committee, well after the Senate had received the nomination, instead of immediately upon receipt of the nomination. Nonetheless, such concerns might be addressed in any agreement to expedite the confirmation process for nominations qualifying as privileged nominations (including requiring more than one Senator to object to a nomination being listed on the *Calendar* as a privileged nomination).

Treat District Court Nominations Differently than Circuit Court Nominations

Another option the Senate might consider is to treat, during various stages of the confirmation process, district court nominations differently than circuit court nominations. One proposal rests on the premise that the "best mechanism to relieve the mounting pressure on the district courts is to decouple the district judge nomination process from the deeply politicized circuit court nomination process"[58] and that "the whole problem with district judges is that the process has been bound up with practices for circuit judges."[59]

Along these lines, the proposal includes three specific changes that might shorten the time from nomination to confirmation for district court nominees.[60] First, the Senate could, for district court nominees, streamline the Judiciary Committee questionnaire so that it is mostly limited to questions related to the nominee's legal experience. The rationale underlying this proposed change is that, arguably, the only consequential questions for a district court nominee are those describing cases that the nominee decided as a judge or handled as a lawyer.[61] Additionally, such questions would still require nominees to provide contact information for judges and counsel involved with the cases on which they have worked.[62]

Second, the Senate could eliminate routine committee hearings on district court nominations. The rationale behind this change is that "the hearing generally has served to bog down progress through the Committee of unobjectionable district judge nominations. And, even when both sides have good will in moving nominations forward, the hearing is the variable that injects most uncertainty into the confirmation schedule."[63] Instead, "[w]ithout a hearing, a committee rule could be set with a minimum referral time to the Committee of sixty or ninety days, to be followed by a vote at the next business meeting (or whenever the blue slips have been returned, whichever is later) absent exceptional circumstances in which the majority and minority agree that a special hearing or investigation is required."[64]

As the proposal emphasizes, this would be very similar to the process by which nominees to U.S. attorney positions are considered by the Judiciary Committee. Like district court judges, U.S. attorneys, it has been argued, "are key officers in the day-to-day operations of the federal legal system. Yet they receive no hearing, ordinary issues are handled promptly, and nominees are reported speedily."[65] The primary defense of retaining the hearing, it is suggested, "is the opportunity of a conscientious Senator to impress upon nominees the importance of genuine issues of law."[66] However, the proposal considers the "odds that the hearing becomes just another tool of delay are overwhelming,"[67] outweighing the need for Senators to emphasize particular concerns or issues to district court nominees.[68]

Finally, the proposal emphasizes expediting floor consideration of district court nominations. To this end, it would amend Senate rules to ensure a vote on such nominations shortly after being reported by the Judiciary Committee. One possible way to expedite the process is for the majority leader to be given the privilege "after a district judge nomination has laid over on the floor for one week, to call for an 'expedited' confirmation vote under a procedure requiring some higher threshold—perhaps the greater of sixty Senators or three-quarters of those present and voting. Nominations meeting the threshold would be confirmed; others would be returned to the Senate *Executive Calendar* for consideration under current rules, by unanimous consent or invocation of cloture."[69] Such a procedure might be useful in reducing the leverage individual Senators have when they withhold their consent to proceed to a district court nomination (particularly those considered uncontroversial), an issue that some Senators have considered especially problematic in recent years.[70]

One possible concern with the above proposals for treating district court nominations differently than circuit court nominations is that they are modest in nature (and, thus, may not succeed in significantly reducing the amount of time from nomination to confirmation for many, if not most, district court nominees). Additionally, Senators might consider routine hearings for district court nominees to be of value and, thus, might be reluctant to eliminate them altogether.[71]

CONCLUSION

The Senate, if it determines that the lengthening judicial confirmation process is a problem, might consider various policy options to shorten the process. The Senate, for example, could create time frames for one or more stages of the confirmation process by establishing deadlines for acting on a nomination. Such time frames might have the effect of shortening the confirmation process for judicial nominees as well as standardizing (as much as possible) the process across presidencies. Some potential drawbacks of using time frames include the issue of enforcement (i.e., what happens if a time frame is not followed?) as well as giving the President greater leverage or influence in the selection of judicial nominees.

The Senate might also fast-track certain nominations. Some nominations, for example, might be classified as "privileged" nominations and, thus, be acted upon by the Senate in a relatively expedited manner. Such privileged nominations might include U.S. district court nominations for vacancies considered judicial emergencies and/or nominations considered uncontroversial. There might, however, be some drawbacks to fast-tracking some nominations, including the concern of some Members in preserving the role of the Judiciary Committee in having its say on every judicial nomination submitted by the President.

Finally, the Senate might treat district court nominations differently than circuit court nominations by streamlining the Judiciary Committee questionnaire for district court nominees, eliminating routine committee hearings for district court nominees, and expediting floor consideration of district court nominees by adopting an amendment to Senate rules that would ensure a vote on such nominations shortly after being reported by the Judiciary Committee. While treating district court nominations differently than circuit court nominations might make sense given differences in the nature of the work done by trial judges versus appellate judges, Senators might, for various reasons, be reluctant to change the process for district court nominees (e.g., Senators might consider routine hearings for district court nominees as valuable in assessing nominees' professional competence or temperament).

End Notes

[1] Specifically, nominations to the U.S. courts of appeals and U.S. district courts. As discussed in the text, U.S. district courts are the federal trial courts of general jurisdiction while the U.S.

circuit courts of appeals take appeals from U.S. district courts and are also empowered to review the decisions of many administrative agencies.

[2] During the 112th Congress, for example, Senator Patrick J. Leahy of Vermont criticized the wait time for President Obama's judicial nominees as generally being much too long. In July 2012, Senator Leahy stated that the treatment of President Obama's nominees had "amounted to months of unnecessary delays" and that the Senate minority had engaged in "across-the-board stalling of judicial nominees," which he said had "led to the backlog in confirmations" and "months of delays" for certain nominees. Sen. Patrick J. Leahy, "Executive Session," Remarks in the Senate, Congressional Record, daily edition, July 10, 2012, p. S.4801. Senator Chuck Grassley has disputed the argument that President Obama's nominees have been treated differently by the Senate, stating "[b]y any objective measure, this President has been treated fairly and consistent with past Senate practice." Sen. Chuck Grassley, "Executive Session," Remarks in the Senate, Congressional Record, daily edition, July 10, 2012, p.S4803.

[3] See CRS Report R41942, Vacancies on Article III District and Circuit Courts, 1977-2011: Data, Causes, and Implications, by Denis Steven Rutkus.

[4] The "average" or "mean" is the arithmetic mean (both terms are used interchangeably throughout this report), while the "median" indicates the middle value for a particular set of numbers. In this case, the middle value for the number of days from nomination to confirmation for all circuit or district court nominees whose nominations were approved by the Senate during a President's tenure in office.

[5] A prior analysis by CRS has shown that the increase in average and median waiting times from nomination to confirmation for U.S. circuit and district court nominees includes the waiting times for nominees who are considered uncontroversial and receive bipartisan support among Senators. See CRS Report R42732, Length of Time from Nomination to Confirmation for "Uncontroversial" U.S. Circuit and District Court Nominees: Detailed Analysis, by Barry J. McMillion.

[6] One Senator has described the judicial confirmation process as "badly broken" and argued that delays in the confirmation process should be the exception rather than the rule, stating that "some delay in the Senate's judicial confirmation may be necessary from time to time. If, for whatever reason, a majority of Senators needs more time to determine whether a particular nominee deserves confirmation, a short delay may be appropriate." Senator John Cornyn, "Our Broken Judicial Confirmation Process and the Need for Filibuster Reform," Harvard Journal of Law & Public Policy, vol. 27 (2003-04), pp. 183, 187.

[7] Senator Chuck Grassley has argued, for example, that "the Senate must not place quantity confirmed over quality confirmed. These lifetime appointments are too important to the Federal judiciary and the American people to simply rubber stamp them." Sen. Chuck Grassley, "Executive Session," Remarks in the Senate, Congressional Record, daily edition, October 13, 2011, p. S.6487. Similarly, Senator Jeff Sessions has stated that the Senate "need[s] to take time to look at nominees and ask the tough questions. We are not a rubberstamp." Sen. Jeff Sessions, "Executive Session," Remarks in the Senate, Congressional Record, daily edition, November 9, 2009, p. S11275. And, finally, as one scholar has stated "[i]t is neither surprising nor wrong that conflict over decisions to appoint particular individuals has emerged. Life tenure is a rare event in any democracy, and those selected and confirmed to serve must, therefore, be individuals in whom confidence is shared." Judith Resnik, "Judicial Selection and Democratic Theory: Demand, Supply, and Life Tenure," Cardozo Law Review, vol. 26 (2004-05), p. 631 (hereinafter Resnik, "Judicial Selection and Democratic Theory").

[8] Pursuant to this constitutional language, Article III judges may hold office for as long as they live or until they voluntarily leave office. A President has no power to remove them from office. Article III judges, however, may be removed by Congress through the process of impeachment by the House and conviction by the Senate.

[9] While American Samoa is an overseas territory of the United States, it does not have a federal district court and has not been incorporated into a federal judicial district. The High Court of American Samoa is the court of general jurisdiction for the territory. The High Court has limited jurisdiction to hear cases under particular federal statutes. See Michael W. Weaver, "The Territory Federal Jurisdiction Forgot: The Question Of Greater Federal Jurisdiction In American Samoa," Pacific Rim Law & Policy Journal Association, vol. 17 (March 2008), p. 325.

[10] The length of time it takes a judicial nominee, once nominated, to be confirmed by the Senate depends (in part) on the length of time the nominee waits for a committee hearing, the length of time until his or her nomination is reported, and the length of time it remains on the Executive Calendar prior to being considered by the full Senate. These stages of the confirmation process are more fully discussed in CRS Report R43058, President Obama's First-Term U.S. Circuit and District Court Nominations: An Analysis and Comparison with Presidents Since Reagan, by Barry J. McMillion.

[11] As stated previously, the "average" or "mean" is the arithmetic mean (both terms are used interchangeably throughout this report), while the "median" indicates the middle value for a particular set of numbers. In this case, the middle value for the number of days from nomination to confirmation for all circuit or district court nominees whose nominations were approved by the Senate during a President's tenure in office.

[12] For a discussion on the background and types of holds, see CRS Report 98-712, "Holds" in the Senate, by Walter J. Oleszek. The use of anonymous holds, especially by Senators belonging to the minority party, has received particular attention in recent years. Norman Ornstein has argued that "the use of holds to block multiple nominations for not weeks or months but years or until death, were not typical [in the past]; now they are the standard. Democrats were mischief-makers in the George W. Bush years; Republicans in the Barack Obama years have become recidivist hard-core offenders." "Shame on the Senate for Confirmation Games," Roll Call, Dec. 14, 2011, p. 22.

[13] For further discussion of factors that influence the confirmation process generally, see CRS Report R43058, President Obama's First-Term U.S. Circuit and District Court Nominations: An Analysis and Comparison with Presidents Since Reagan, by Barry J. McMillion. See also Logan Dancey, Kjersten R. Nelson, and Eve M. Ringsmuth, "'Strict Scrutiny?' The Content of Senate Judicial Confirmation Hearings during the George W. Bush Administration," Judicature, vol. 95 (Nov./Dec. 2011), p. 128.

[14] The number of circuit court nominees whose nominations were confirmed by the Senate ranged from a high of 83 during the Reagan presidency to a low of 39, thus far, during the Obama presidency.

[15] Note that the median, or middle value for the nominees, is less affected by outliers or extreme cases, i.e., nominees whose elapsed time from first nomination to confirmation was unusually long or short.

[16] The fact that the mean number of days for President G.W. Bush's circuit court nominees is approximately 135 days longer than the median number of days for the same group of nominees suggests that there was a group of nominees whose nominations were approved by the Senate after relatively lengthy periods of time after first being nominated as compared with the nominations of President G.W. Bush's other circuit court nominees. For

example, approximately 23% of President G.W. Bush's circuit court nominees waited more than 500 days from first nomination to confirmation while nearly half (48%) waited less than 200 days from first nomination to confirmation.

[17] The number of district court nominees whose nominations were confirmed by the Senate ranged from a high of 307 during the Clinton presidency to a low of 150 during the G.H.W. Bush presidency.

[18] President Obama is the only President of these five for whom, during his time in office, U.S. circuit and district court nominees waited, both in terms of average and median number of days, more than half of a calendar year (i.e., more than 182 days) to be confirmed after being nominated.

[19] Note that circuit court nominations are not affected by the new standing order.

[20] As one observer noted, prior to the new standing order, "even where the sixty votes required by Rule XXII can be mustered, a successful cloture vote comes with its own cost in the form of thirty hours of debate time that the minority can force even after cloture has been invoked. Just a few dozen nominees would mean hundreds of hours of post-cloture floor time. In a busy Congress ... the Majority Leader does not have that much time available to spend." Michael L. Shenkman, "Decoupling District from Circuit Judge Nominations: A Proposal to Put Trial Bench Confirmations on Track," Arkansas Law Review, vol. 65 (2012), pp. 295 (hereinafter Shenkman, "Decoupling District from Circuit Judge Nominations").

[21] Sen. Harry Reid, Remarks in the Senate, Congressional Record, daily edition, January 24, 2013, p.S272.

[22] For further discussion of the standing order in effect for the 113th Congress, see CRS Report R42996, Changes to Senate Procedures in the 113th Congress Affecting the Operation of Cloture (S.Res. 15 and S.Res. 16), by Elizabeth Rybicki.

[23] See, for example, Shenkman, "Decoupling District from Circuit Judge Nominations," pp. 229-31; Vicki C. Jackson, "Packages of Judicial Independence: The Selection and Tenure of Article III Judges," Georgetown Law Journal, vol. 95 (2006-07), p. 979 (hereinafter Jackson, "Packages of Judicial Independence"); Michael Teter, "Rethinking Consent: Proposals for Reforming the Judicial Confirmation Process," Ohio State Law Journal, vol. 73 (2012), pp. 297-99; Karl A. Schweitzer, "Litigating the Appointments Clause: The Most Effective Solution for Senate Obstruction of the Judicial Confirmation Process," University of Pennsylvania Journal of Constitutional Law, vol. 12 (Mar. 2010), p. 915; Sarah A. Binder and Forrest Maltzman, Advice and Dissent: The Struggle to Shape the Federal Bench and Why it Matters (Washington, DC: Brookings Institution Press, 2009), pp. 127-42 (hereinafter "Advice & Dissent").

[24] The Judicial Conference of the United States is the principal policymaking body concerned with the administration of the U.S. Courts. The Conference defines a "judicial emergency" for a circuit court vacancy as any vacancy in a court of appeals where adjusted case filings per appellate panel are in excess of 700 or any vacancy that is in existence more than 18 months where adjusted filings are between 500 to 700 per panel. For district court vacancies, a judicial emergency exists when a district court has weighted filings in excess of 600 per judgeship; or a vacancy is in existence more than 18 months where weighted filings are between 430 to 600 per judgeship; or any district court with more than one authorized judgeship and only one active judge. A list of vacancies considered "judicial emergencies" by the Judicial Conference is available on the U.S. Courts website at http://www. uscourts.gov/JudgesAndJudgeships/ JudicialVacancies/JudicialEmergencies.aspx. The president of the American Bar Association has suggested that judicial emergencies are now more prevalent because of the length of time it takes for the Senate to confirm judicial

nominees. See Laurel Bellows, "Judicial emergencies worsen as partisanship stalls nominations in the Senate," President's Message (July 1, 2013), online at http://www.abajournal.com/magazine/article/judicial_emergencies_worsen_as_partisanship_stalls_nominations_in_the_senat.

[25] CRS Report R41942, Vacancies on Article III District and Circuit Courts, 1977-2011: Data, Causes, and Implications, by Denis Steven Rutkus. The report notes, for example, that "throughout most of the 111th Congress, the effective vacancy rate in the district courts was well above the historically high benchmark of 10.6%, reaching as high as 13.6% near the end of the Congress."

[26] See CRS Report R43058, President Obama's First-Term U.S. Circuit and District Court Nominations: An Analysis and Comparison with Presidents Since Reagan, by Barry J. McMillion.

[27] As displayed in Figure 1, President Obama's district court nominees have waited, both in terms of the average and median number of days, more than 200 days from nomination to confirmation.

[28] Caseload statistics for U.S. circuit and district court can be accessed at http://www.uscourts.gov/Statistics/ FederalJudicialCaseloadStatistics.aspx.

[29] Chief Justice John G. Roberts, Jr., "2010 Year-End Report on the Federal Judiciary," Jan. 2011, http://www.supremecourt.gov/publicinfo/year-end/2010year-endreport.pdf.

[30] Ibid.

[31] Chief Justice William Rehnquist, "1997 Year-End Report on the Federal Judiciary," Third Branch, Jan. 1998.

[32] Chief Justice William H. Rehnquist: In His Own Words, Third Branch, Sept. 2005, http://www.uscourts.gov/news/ TheThirdBranch/05-09-01/Chief_Justice_William_H_Rehnquist_In_His_Own_Words.aspx.

[33] Chief Justice William Rehnquist, "2001 Year-End Report on the Federal Judiciary," Jan. 2002, http://www.supremecourt.gov/publicinfo/year-end/2001year-endreport.aspx.

[34] Shenkman, "Decoupling District from Circuit Court Nominations," p. 297.

[35] This might be particularly true given other trends related to the federal judiciary, such as stagnant judicial salaries and an increase in caseloads. As Russell Wheeler has noted, "the changes that make the job less attractive than it was several years ago elevate the importance of a selection process that is not itself an impediment that discourages good people from considering federal judicial service." "Is Our Dysfunctional Process for Filling Judicial Vacancies an Insoluble Problem?", Jan. 2013, p. 8, http://www.acslaw.org/sites/default/files/Wheeler_- _Filling_Judicial_Vacancies.pdf (hereinafter Wheeler, "Dysfunctional Process").

[36] Judge Carolyn D. King, "Hallows Lecture: Challenges to Judicial Independence and the Rule of Law: A Perspective from the Circuit Courts," Marquette Law Review, vol. 90 (2007), p. 782.

[37] Nicholas Katzenbach, Some Of It Was Fun: Working With RFK and LBJ, (New York, NY: Norton, 2008), pp. 60-61, cited in Shenkman, "Decoupling District from Circuit Court Nominations," p. 228. Shenkman himself states "[t]rial judges require judgment about the care and feeding of the cases on their docket—and of litigants and their lawyers. They must answer many legal questions without political roots," p. 228.

[38] Jackson, "Packages of Judicial Independence," p. 985.

[39] Ibid.

[40] These proposals might also contribute to making the time from nomination to confirmation more uniform across different presidencies, irrespective of variations occurring in the

partisan composition of the Senate. As one scholar has noted, however, the current confirmation "process may not be amenable to a 'solution' if that means a return to the days of prompt and virtually controversy-free confirmations," and it might be the case that "confirmations measured in days after nominations, rather than months" are unlikely to return any time soon. Wheeler, "Dysfunctional Process," p. 4. The difficulty, in part, in adopting any reforms intended to reduce the amount of time from nomination to confirmation is because "[w]ith the perceived stakes of judicial appointments high, the minority party is unlikely to agree to any procedural reform that diminishes its existing ability to influence the course of advice and consent." Sarah Binder, "Advice and Consent for Judicial Nominations: Can the President and the Senate Do Better?", March 2009, p. 28, http://www.wilsoncenter.org/sites/default/files/Binder.pdf (hereinafter Binder, "Advice and Consent").

[41] One such proposal is the creation of a single-issue office within the White House concerned only with judicial nominations, similar to the Council on Environmental Quality or the Office of National Drug Policy. David Fontana, "Judging Obama's Second Term," Huffington Post, Nov. 14, 2012, http://www.huffingtonpost.com/david-fontana/ obama-judicial-appointments-2nd-term_b_2131912.html. Presumably such an office might reduce the amount of time it takes a President to nominate individuals to vacant judgeships by making more efficient the selection and vetting of nominees. Additionally, the New York Times has editorialized that nominees should be recommended by Senators within 60 days of a vacancy and the White House and Justice Department should nominate candidates within 60 days of receiving such recommendations. "Judges Needed for Federal Courts," New York Times, Dec. 12, 2012, http://www.nytimes.com/2012/12/13/opinion/judges-needed-for-federal-courts.html.

[42] For a comprehensive discussion of other reform proposals see Mitchel A. Sollenberger, Judicial Appointments and Democratic Controls (Durham, NC: Carolina Academic Press, 2011), pp. 157-186.

[43] President G.W. Bush also proposed that Presidents submit judicial nominations to the Senate within 180 days of receiving notice of a federal court vacancy or intended retirement. President George W. Bush, "Remarks by the President on Judicial Nominations," October 30, 2002, http://georgewbush-whitehouse.archives.gov/news/releases/ 2002/10/20021030-6.html.

[44] Ibid.

[45] President Barack Obama, "Remarks by the President in the State of the Union Address," Jan. 24, 2012, http://www.whitehouse.gov/the-press-office/2012/01/24/remarks-President-state-union-address.

[46] Another proposal by two law professors, Michael Gerhardt and Richard Painter, includes time tables for Senate action on nominations. The two propose (i) Senate hearings being scheduled within 90 days of when the President sends the nomination to the Senate; (ii) the end of using anonymous holds to delay committee or full Senate action on the nomination; instead, the Senate would accommodate brief delays of up to 30 days for a committee or floor vote if a Senator, with the support of one other Senator, states a good reason for the delay, and why his or her concerns could have not been addressed earlier; and (iii) once a judicial nominee is reported out of committee, the presumption in the Senate should be that a majority of "yes" votes are needed to confirm the nominee. In rare cases, Senators objecting to a vote would be permitted to introduce a resolution stating with specificity their objections to the nomination, and if the resolution received a specific number of affirmative votes in support of it (e.g., at least 45) from other Senators, it would delay a final up-or-

down confirmation vote on the nomination for a specified period of time, perhaps until the next session of Congress after which there would be an up-or-down vote with no further delay. See Michael Gerhardt & Richard Painter, "'Extraordinary Circumstances:' The Legacy of the Gang of 14 and a Proposal for Judicial Nominations Reform," November 2011, pp. 6-7, http://www.acslaw.org/sites/default/files/Gerhardt-Painter_- _Extraordinary_ Circumstances.pdf.

[47] Senator Arlen Specter, S.Res. 327, "A resolution providing for a protocol for nonpartisan confirmation of judicial nominees," introduced on April 1, 2004, https://www.govtrack. us/congress/bills/108/sres327.

[48] One bipartisan proposal, by a Miller Center Commission, called on the Senate to act even more quickly on judicial nominations. The Commission stated that the "Senate Judiciary Committee and the Senate should clear nominees for full Senate confirmation within two months [or approximately 60 days] of receiving the president's nomination." Miller Center Commission No. 7, "Report of the Commission on the Selection of Federal Judges," 1996, p. 9, http://web1.millercenter.org/commissions/comm_1996.pdf (hereinafter "Miller Center Report"). The Commission included members such as former Attorney General Nicholas Katzenbach; former Senator (and Majority Leader) Howard H. Baker, Jr.; former Senator Birch Bayh, Jr.; former White House Counsel Lloyd N. Cutler; and former White House Counsel Fred F. Fielding.

[49] CRS Report RS21506, Implications for the Senate of President Bush's Proposal on Judicial Nominations, by Betsy Palmer.

[50] Sarah A. Binder and Forrest Maltzman, "Advice & Dissent," pp. 147-48; Binder, "Advice and Consent," p. 28.

[51] For further discussion, see CRS Report RL34405, Role of Home State Senators in the Selection of Lower Federal Court Judges, by Denis Steven Rutkus.

[52] Wheeler, "Dysfunctional Process," p. 13.

[53] For further discussion, see CRS Report R41872, Presidential Appointments, the Senate's Confirmation Process, and Changes Made in the 112th Congress, by Maeve P. Carey. Some of the information presented above in the section "Fast-track certain nominations" is taken from this report.

[54] The process might be expedited for such nominations because the committee would no longer need to hold a hearing on the nomination (as is the current practice for every circuit and district court nomination), and it would not need to schedule executive business meetings for the purpose of reporting privileged nominations to the full Senate.

[55] Providing a privileged status for at least some district court nominations would reflect long-standing Senate tradition on deferring to a district court nominee's home-state Senators in determining whether a nominee is approved by the full Senate. Senator Sheldon Whitehouse, for example, has stated that "there is a tradition in this body that while circuit court nominees are considered what one might call, for better or worse, political fair game, there has been a tradition of courtesy and comity regarding district court judges who sit in the Senator's home state when both of the home state Senators have agreed to and accepted the President's recommendations and supported it, given their blue slip to the committee and so forth." "Unanimous Consent Request—Executive Calendar," Remarks in the Senate, Congressional Record, daily edition, Aug. 5, 2010, p.S6971. Additionally, many district court nominations receive little or no opposition, as measured by the number of "nay" votes received, when they are approved by the Senate. During the 112th Congress, for example, 63 of 99 district court nominations (or 64%) were approved by voice vote or a unanimous roll call vote. Such a proposal might help expedite Senate processing of nominations such

as these, which had little or no opposition. For further discussion and analysis of Senate approval of uncontroversial judicial nominees, see CRS Report R42732, Length of Time from Nomination to Confirmation for "Uncontroversial" U.S. Circuit and District Court Nominees: Detailed Analysis, by Barry J. McMillion.

[56] Which specific nominations would qualify as privileged nominations might be determined as a result of negotiations among the chair of the Judiciary Committee, the Majority Leader, and the Minority Leader.

[57] As with S.Res. 116, such a process for judicial nominations would not apply to the nomination if any Senator objects to it. In those cases, the nomination would revert back to the regular confirmation process (i.e., by being referred to the Senate Judiciary Committee).

[58] Shenkman, "Decoupling District from Circuit Judge Nominations," p. 224.

[59] Ibid., p. 298.

[60] Given the scope of this report, one change suggested for the pre-nomination stage of the confirmation process is not discussed. Specifically, an "Administration could modestly mitigate the powerful force of delay in the bargaining dynamic with Senators over district judge vacancies by publishing the status of pre-nomination negotiations, although not the names of the nominees themselves." In short, the Administration would have a "nomination status page" that would indicate whether the White House had received nominee recommendations from Senators. Shenkman, "Decoupling District from Circuit Judge Nominations," pp. 299-300.

[61] Ibid., p. 303.

[62] The Miller Center Commission report also recommended reforming or shortening the questionnaire (including for circuit court nominees) stating that "the Senate Judiciary Committee should explore whether or not it is really necessary or appropriate to obtain all the information presently sought." Miller Center Report, p. 9.

[63] Shenkman, "Decoupling District from Circuit Judge Nominations," p. 305.

[64] Ibid., p. 306.

[65] Ibid.

[66] Ibid., p. 307.

[67] Ibid., pp. 307-08.

[68] Any new procedure that eliminated hearings for district court nominees could, of course, include a provision that requires the Judiciary Committee to conduct a hearing for a district court nominee if requested by any Senator.

[69] Ibid., p. 309.

[70] Senator Leahy, for example, has stated that during the 111th Congress, the Senate had "wasted weeks and months having to seek time agreements in order to consider nominations that were reported by the Senate Judiciary Committee unanimously and who are then confirmed overwhelmingly by the Senate once they are finally allowed to be considered." "Executive Session," Remarks in the Senate, Congressional Record, daily edition, March 2, 2010, p. S .906.

[71] One scholar notes that, for hearings conducted on lower federal court nominations, "the quality and depth of oral questioning varies widely." He also discusses, however, reasons why Senators might nonetheless be reluctant to eliminate hearings for circuit and district court nominees, including using hearings to assess a nominee's professional competence, personal integrity, temperament, political philosophies, and judicial management skills. In terms of the last factor, judicial management skills, he argues that "[s]ome of the most substantive exchanges between Senators and nominees have concerned issues of judicial management" rather than issues related to constitutional adjudication or judicial philosophy.

See William G. Ross, "The Questioning Of Lower Federal Court Nominees During The Senate Confirmation Process," William & Mary Bill of Rights Journal, vol. 10 (2001-02), pp. 124-160, 171.

INDEX

D

E

F

G

H

I

J

L

Q

R

S

T

U

V

W